Preferable Futures

Digital Cultures Series

Edited by Andreas Bernard, Armin Beverungen,
Irina Kaldrack, Martina Leeker and Sascha Simons

A book series of the *Centre for Digital Cultures*

Preferable Futures

edited by Irina Kaldrack and Rolf F. Nohr

μ meson press

**Bibliographical Information of the
German National Library**
The German National Library lists this publication in the
Deutsche Nationalbibliografie (German National Bib-
liography); detailed bibliographic information is available
online at http://dnb.d-nb.de.

Published in 2023 by meson press, Lüneburg
www.meson.press

Design concept: Torsten Köchlin, Silke Krieg
Cover image: © Lily Wittenburg
Copy editing: Janet Leyton-Grant
Typesetting assistance: Inga Luchs

The print edition of this book is printed by Lightning Source,
Milton Keynes, United Kingdom.

ISBN (Print):   978-3-95796-033-7
ISBN (PDF):   978-3-95796-034-4
DOI: 10.14619/0337

The digital edition of this publication can be downloaded
freely at: www.meson.press.

Contents

Preferable Futures: An Introduction

Irina Kaldrack and Rolf F. Nohr

The present has made a pressing matter of the future. The crises of the present—climate change, biodiversity crises, the foreseeable scarcity of resources, energy consumption, and (more) pandemics—have thrown human existence, or at least the specific lifestyles we cultivate, into question. One probable future that looms on the horizon is of particular concern: if products continue to be manufactured (by major companies) and consumed (by large numbers of people or in powerful societies) as they currently are, we will reach certain tipping points that will make life on planet Earth impossible, or at least extremely difficult, for the human species.[1] This catastrophic vision calls for action in the present, and in recent years, Fridays for Future, Extinction Rebellion, and other social movements have once more been raising this emphatic demand, a stance that was substantiated in legal terms in March 2021, when the German Federal Constitutional Court issued a judgement confirming that current emission reduction requirements limit future generations' rights

---

1   Forecasts such as these are based on simulations that combine physical and biochemical laws of nature with existing series of measurements in models of the climate. From a mathematical perspective, these models are dynamic systems that depict conditions of balance. When certain parameters change too drastically, the system enters a phase of chaotic behavior, after which it is able to find a new, dynamic balance. In the discourse on climate change, these parameters are known as tipping points. Discourse on climate change, or the climate crisis, draws on simulations that depict various courses of future developments as scenarios; the models assume, for example, that human organisms need certain moderate outside temperatures to maintain a necessary body temperature of approx. 37 degrees Celsius and model the occurrence of "un-realities of life" caused by climate change on this basis. These scenarios have been documented in assessment reports issued by the Intergovernmental Panel on Climate Change (IPCC). The sixth edition was published in August 2021; it describes the current state of natural scientific knowledge on climate change and outlines scenarios for possible further developments.

10 to freedom.[2] This clearly shows how present conditions color our vision of the future, and how this vision in turn informs our actions in the present.[3] This dual reference to the present day applies not only to future disasters but to how we envision, draft, and negotiate preferable futures. In that context, current debates on climate change, on the measures taken to reach the 1.5-degree target, and on subjective lifestyles indicate that matters of distribution and power are at issue here (see Horn 2018). The creation of preferable futures requires negotiation processes that involve many different stakeholders. The basic premise of this book is that any projection of the future by necessity contains both non-knowledge and knowledge, and thus creates action. Accordingly, we cannot expect any one projection of the future to occur, as its prediction alone generates actions that in turn modify it. In this sense, we assume that there cannot truly be just *one* future, only more or less probable, more or less possible futures (from the present perspective). The chapters included here aim to address how envisioning, drafting, and negotiating preferable futures always contains the aforementioned dual reference to the present day (knowledge and non-knowledge, potential practices and excluded actions). We feel it is necessary to reveal and reflect this dual reference (and the production conditions of potential futures) as much as possible—reflecting on the historic genealogy of such productions while doing so. This (also) means focusing on the conflict between current discourse and the situation that arises from this discourse and yet is simultaneously viewed as problematic. What can we do? How can we change things today for a future that we cannot predict

2   Federal Constitutional Court, First Senate Ruling of 24 March 2021, 1 BvR 2656/18, Paragraph 1–270, accessed August 27, 2021, http://www.bverfg.de/e/rs20210324_1bvr265618.html.

3   This type of future orientation is nothing new. It was at the core of Hans Carl von Carlowitz's concept of sustainability as the conservation of resources, as defined in *Sylvicultura Oeconmica* (1713). It has accompanied the formation of environmental consciousness since the 1960s, see for example Rachel Carson's influential book, *Silent Spring* (1962).

with certainty but that we need to envision if we are to (re-)shape
it? The matter of possible futures, probable futures, and preferable futures is the intersection of the different perspectives
collected here. The book is the result of a joint panel entitled
Trans-Formation Design in Digital Cultures, hosted by Saskia
Hebert, Wolfgang Jonas, Irina Kaldrack, and Rolf F. Nohr at the
Digital Cultures: Knowledge/Culture/Technology conference at Leuphana University, Lüneburg in the autumn of 2018. As teachers of
transformation design and media studies (all at the Braunschweig
University of Art at the time), we discussed the relationship of
research to futures and digital cultures in the context of transformation, sustainability, and the Anthropocene. Our shared
point of reference was, and is, the envisioning, drafting, and
negotiating of futures. We asked ourselves how we might create
specific spaces for negotiation where preferable futures can be
negotiated in the first place and how these might have been created in the past. Each of the analyses collected here argues this
matter from a specific perspective and from a different point of
access: Saskia Hebert looks at Braunschweig University of Art's
M.A. in Transformation Design, focusing on the skills that need to
be tested within the program; Wolfgang Jonas focuses on current
discourse in design and how to determine what may constitute
adequate negotiation zones in the spirit of transformation design;
Rolf F. Nohr analyzes historic use cases to show how negotiation
zones carved out by institutions to negotiate futures in particular
are used to practice specific rationalities; and Irina Kaldrack
scrutinizes contemporary theories to question the relationship
between newer epistemologies and the opening up of futures.
The chapters in this book all illuminate aspects of what we have
called negotiation zones for futures. We view these negotiation
zones as experimental and (occasionally) radical areas of activity
that allow us to explore and envision preferable futures through
dialogical and agonistic processes (see Jonas 2014; 2018). For this
precise reason, we believe that these texts, with their different
objects, approaches, and focuses on the production of futures
illustrate ways to potentially forge a link to how we could, and

should, envision, draft, and negotiate preferable futures. On the following pages, we create a framework that is also relevant for other discussions around projections of the future at the intersection of media studies and design. We begin by characterizing (with a consciously critical and dualistic eye) prevalent lines of current discourse captured and discussed in media studies and design. Over the course of the characterization, it becomes quite clear how discourse on digital cultures and sustainability intermeshes with the question of futures: they share historical epistemologies, they use the same concepts to an extent, and they are closely connected when it comes to modelling and simulation practices and the capturing of data. We focus on how our ways of envisioning and drafting futures, as well as how we reflect on these projections of the future, are being conducted in the present. Even though these current lines of discourse are rooted in the epistemes of the early 1970s (and further back), they are currently being reconnected and reconfigured by the dynamics of contemporary media, social and/or technological discourse formations. As a second step, we focus on how we treat projections of the future, and the reference to the future contained therein, to frame the recursive reference to the present day. If projections of the future have a particular impact on our decisions, actions, and manners of behavior in the present, they also affect the relationship between theory and practice, knowledge, and action, which are especially relevant when it comes to designing negotiation zones for futures.

The Present as the Origin of Futures

In light of climate change and digitization, the matter of our future/s, is a pressing one for the (German) public. The advancing automation and autonomization of digital technologies demand that we deal with future ways of working and knowledge cultures; they also call into question traditional definitions of what separates humans from machines, definitions that usually include terms such as "self-moving" and "having a soul." The ecological crises of the present, such as climate change, pollution of our soil and oceans, and the biodiversity crisis, demand that we deal with the lifestyles of individuals and societies and admonish us to meet the needs of other life forms and species in addition to striving for intergenerational and global justice.

From a media scientific perspective, media ecological theories in particular address this interrelationship. On the one hand, media ecological approaches highlight issues such as resource consumption and environmental damage as well as global (social) injustice caused or intensified by digital cultures. These issues begin with the extraction of raw materials needed for infrastructure and devices, and extend through to production conditions for end devices, the environmental impact of digital culture infrastructure energy consumption, recycling, disposal of devices, and affect access to digital cultures as well as the power and economies within them (Gabrys 2013; Parikka 2015; Cubitt 2017). On the other hand, media ecological approaches examine how digital technologies become the environment, in other words, become part of the eco system—capturing it by means of various sensors on different levels—and operate in an increasingly autonomous manner in accordance with different objectives. Examples include (social) platforms, smart assist systems, autonomous driving, optimization of deliveries through self-organized warehouses and route planning, the autonomization of production in agriculture, and the so frequently invoked Industry 4.0: human users embedded in structures in which they cannot fully control the effect of their actions or in which their actions are determined by their surroundings (Taffel 2019). This goes hand in hand with the fact that users are addressed less on a cognitive-semantic level and more on an affective and supposedly intuitive level (Angerer 2017; Rieger 2021). Our physical-digital surroundings have in turn been embedded locally—physically, materially, and tangibly—and simultaneously spread (globally) in the form of infrastructures, technical-algorithmic organization of data processing, and human work. In short, this means that, in media scientific discourse,

14 contemporary digital cultures are characterized by the fact that they appear to be structures in which there is interaction between (communicative and physical) behavior and technical-algorithmic operations. These interactions address affects and intuition and are determined by self-organization, thus embedding human users into material-technological surroundings, whereby said surroundings have been both embedded locally and (at various scales) spread topologically.

This point of view corresponds in particular to contemporary weak ontologies that describe everything in existence as undergoing a process of becoming.[4] Prominent representatives of New Materialism, such as Karen Barad (2007), Rosi Braidotti (2013), Jane Bennett (2010), and Donna Haraway (2016) highlight how matter, subjectivities, power, and knowledge each spawn the other within material-technological-semiotic structures, leading to a decentration of subjectivities that goes hand in hand with a revaluation of the becoming and agency of materiality, things, and objects.[5] Following Foucault, in *Die environmentalitäre Situation* [*The Environmentalitarian Situation*], Erich Hörl (2018) outlines environmentality as the decisive signature of the present and its technologies of government; according to Hörl, "power, the world, subjectivity, knowledge and even thought itself are all characterised to a great extent by environmentalisation and crossed by the vectors of becoming-environmental" (228).[6] For Hörl, becoming environmental is a necessary "speculative category" (243) of the necessary reimagining of the creation of

4   On the similarities between digital cultures and weak ontologies, particularly in view of relationality, non-knowledge, and intuition, see Leeker (2021) and Rieger (2021).

5   The authors mentioned above, for example, are partly rooted in the tradition of a feminist philosophy of science and science-technology studies. The actor-network theory can also be characterized as a weak ontology, see Conradi, Derwanz, and Muhle (2013) and Löffler (2018).

6   All quotes translated from German by the authors unless otherwise specified.

the world.[7] Environmentality, relationality, and processuality are dominant signatures of a mélange of differing aspects of discourse that are equally characteristic of how media studies and design deal with pressing questions of the present and future. As an analytical-narrative method, speculation promises to break down one's own patterns of thought; to cross knowledge regimes in opposition to their basic assumptions and blind spots; to assume hidden genealogies of the present and envision new futures, all under the condition of one's own entanglement in power and knowledge regimes and in the knowledge of how they came to be.[8] However, and this is a decisive aspect, methods of speculation—particularly statistical data analysis and scenarios (and the analysis thereof) as well as creative techniques of designing (technological) innovation—have been deeply woven into the technical-algorithmic fundamentals of digital cultures and are a key element of technologies of government, in particular in the shape of risk assessments.[9]

This characterization is reminiscent of the historic constellation of discourses, practices, and technological developments and/ or the realization thereof in the early 1970s. This mélange of differing aspects is characterized by the popularity of cybernetic models, which has been dominated by the intermeshing of logical calculations, (Shannon's) information theory and feedback concepts since its beginnings (Pias 2004). In the 1950s, these

7   Hörl (2018) outlines a new environmentality in a genealogy of thought. He emphasizes that the kind of power and capital that corresponds to environmentality aims to modulate the relationship between humans and their environment, primarily at the level of perception and behavioral control. His plea for a speculative reimagining of the creation of the world refers to Donna Haraway's *Staying with the Trouble* and her notion of sympoiesis as a becoming-with, a process of becoming through relationships and cooperation, which the world (and human beings) produce in the first place.

8   On the origins and/or meaning of speculation in feminist theory movements, see Angerer and Gramlich (2020).

9   On the reciprocal relationship between statistical ways of thinking, risks and technologies of government, see Desrosières (1998), Beck (1986) and recently Amoore (2013).

 theories and concepts promised to model, predict, and control a range of phenomena that can be described through feedback processes—including management and education, along with computers, organisms, and societies. In the 1960s, cybernetic discourse shifted towards complexity, emergence, and self-organization. Precisely because cybernetics ceases to question the fundamental and detailed understanding of complex systems by breaking them down into distinct operators, and instead shows an interest in describing overarching conditions (input and output), they are appealing as a way of examining phenomena on the borders of (non-)decidability. Unpredictability and (un)foreseeability—traditionally complex problems—are reinterpreted as problems which, while still complex, can now be managed with the tools of cybernetics using concepts of self-organization and emergence. One recurring statement explains that while some problems are easier to understand (they can be derived from logical calculations), it is better to approach more complex problems by reproducing (simulating) them.[10] Computer simulations are especially relevant when it comes to modelling natural phenomena (e.g., weather forecasts). These phenomena in particular are formalized as a system of differential equations that model changes in the behavior of reciprocal parameters (such as temperature and pressure). In the 1960s, the mathematical concept of dynamic systems was negotiated in an interdisciplinary context between mathematicians, physicists, chemists, and biologists with regard to the relationship between predictability and unpredictability, order and instability.[11]

10   This statement can be found in the drafts of John von Neumann's automata theory from around 1950, for example (1966, 51), as well as in the examinations of simple, cellular automata conducted by mathematician Stanislaw Ulam ([1952] 1974, 328). On the reconstruction of these works with regard to the limits of predictabilities, see the section "Zelluläre Automaten: Berechenbarkeit zwischen Spiel und Bild" ("Cellular Automata: Predictability between Games and Images") in Kaldrack (2011), in particular 125–36.
11   Aubin and Dahan Dalmedico (2002) provide an overview of developments from a mathematical-historic perspective, with a focus on the genealogy of chaos theory, which became popular in the 1980s.

"General system theory" (Bertalanffy 1968) approaches link these discourses and formalizations of theoretical biology discourses, which in turn provide a key basis for our understanding of nature as an ecological system (e.g. Sprenger 2019). Especially in the field of planning, and against the backdrop of the Cold War, models were developed on the basis of mathematical game theory and operations research.[12] In political consultation in particular, these are flanked by newly developed methods, e.g. scenario analysis (Kahn 1970; Leeker 2020), with system analytics and system dynamics (e.g. Forrester 1968; Beer 1962). In particular, these aim to create a basis, or space, for decisions that have to be made in conditions of uncertainty and/or in which information is incomplete. This interplay of technological developments, discourse, and technologies of government gives rise to epistemological shifts that aim at "speculative implementability" and "feasibility" (Leeker 2020, 166) and operate on the basis of short- and medium-term computer simulated forecasts.[13]

The early 1970s, on the other hand, gave rise to epistemological shifts with a different emphasis. These can in turn be characterized by environmentality, relationality, and processuality, and to an extent employ systemic concepts, however, they are grouped around the notion of the problem or the problematic (Leistert and Schrickel 2021). The protests of 1968 opposed (global) power structures and societal injustice. Civil rights movements against racism and social injustice, pacifist, feminist, anti-capitalist, anti-fascist, and anti-colonial movements, early environmental and anti-nuclear movements, youths and counter-cultures demanded personal and societal civil rights and liberties, political participation, and new moral standards in societal ordinances and

12   Another succinct example worth mentioning is Jay Forrester's system dynamics, which was a decisive factor on which the Club of Rome's *Limits to Growth* concept was based (see Nohr 2019 and the chapter by Nohr in this book).

13   Vehlken (2014) characterizes this epistemology as "hypothesisity" (with reference to Germany's "fast breeder" nuclear reactor developer and lobbyist Wolf Häferle).

 political decision-making processes. Social scientists, humanities scholars, and philosophers (of science) reflected on the non-neutral ways their disciplines constructed both knowledge and history. This context has given rise to other forms of futurology which are participative and empowering, such as Paulo Freire's *Pedagogy of the Oppressed* and Robert Jungk's Future Workshops method (see Schrickel 2021). For approaches like these, problems are no longer "some kind of placeholder for the time span needed to find the solution" (50–1); but are considered a point of entry for debate: "Problems are actively constructed as matters of concern in order to intervene in the present and to create agency and images of change" (51).

With regard to the present as the origin of futures, it is safe to say that environmentality, processuality, and relationality are not just relevant today, they already were at least fifty years ago. In short, natural and engineering sciences are linked to technologies of government in a way that seems aimed at bringing the future to a halt: in current projections, which are largely based on historic processes and (measurable) experiences, probabilities become all the more probable due to the simple fact that the unknown is extrapolated from the past. In this respect, conclusions drawn from the past present are extrapolated to the future; these reflect back on the present in the form of self-fulfilling prophecies, so to speak. The contingency and uncertainty of future developments is either negated or made invisible in residual risk assessments. In the concept of open futures, however, futures are something unpredictable and largely unplannable, but also something that can and should be envisioned, imagined, and shaped in participatory processes. Envisioning and imagining futures always implies—as this cursory depiction shows—a *specificity* of relevance. Projections of the future are furthermore very specifically linked to the relationship between knowledge and non-knowledge—in other words: theory on the one hand and practice on the other.

Our projections of the future are recursive. They are founded in the present and aimed at the present in that they frame present decisions, actions, and behaviors in reference to an envisioned future—at least implicitly. By asking who is referring to the future of what, and what futures are opened or closed therein, the many references to the future can be simplified.

Rüdiger Graf and Benjamin Herzog (2016) have identified four kinds of futures: futures of expectation, creation, risk, and conservation. This differentiation allows us to look at the plurality of contexts, actors, and intentions that dominate the respective visions and creations of futures. This classification also helps us systematize and describe the respective resulting lines of conflict.

Following Rainhart Koselleck's (2004) conceptual pairing of "spaces of experience" and "horizons of expectation"[14]—and in contrast to the same—Graf and Herzog characterize futures of expectation as "the link between a target vision defined in normative terms, a movement index ideally depicting linear progress and, above all, certainty of the expected outcome" (Graf and Herzog 2016, 504–6). But, they continue, there is more than just one future of expectation. Different societies and rationalities have different, plural futures of expectation— and subsequently different assessments of the respective futures. Euphoric views of the future and the belief in progress,

---

14   In his influential 1979 study titled *Futures Past: On the Semantics of Historical Time*, Koselleck explores the concept of historical time on the basis of historical texts: "To be more precise, texts were sought out and interrogated that, explicitly or implicitly, deal with the relation of a given past to a given future" (2004, 3). Koselleck views experience/spaces of experience and expectations/horizons of expectation as meta-historical categories of historical time, the relationship of which is specific to the respective historic time. With the onset of the modern era and the societal and technological revolutions between 1750 and 1850, experience and expectation diverge in the sense of time but are put in a positive relationship to one another in the notion of progress (255–75).

 societal-political utopias and (ecological) apocalypses—to name just a few of the twentieth century's paradigmatic futures of expectation—have been announced and renounced, criticized and celebrated in different contexts and at different times.

Graf and Herzog's second futures category, futures of creation, are particularly relevant when it comes to the paradigms of planning from the 1960s onward:

> We neither expect nor hope for futures of creation, they are instead defined and determined. They are not described and presented, they are decided. In the course of being decided, they follow institutional rather than historic-philosophical rationalities to a great extent. (508)

But this way of approaching futures of creation is found not just in institutional and highly operational areas of society but in a broader sense as well, in the common-sense rationalities of civil society, and as such also shapes various forms of subjective and individual internalization.

Graf and Herzog's third future type, futures of risk, references security and precautions, and is based on the probability of occurrence:

> The aim here is not to live looking towards an expected certainty but to prepare for the unexpected or even the feared. Strictly speaking, calculation has replaced expectation. The willingness that is thus created is not that of someone who is contributing, participating, realizing, as is the case in the activist futures of creation, but of someone who is prepared and on standby. (511)

As a mode of governance, this corresponds to a way of thinking that views defense as the best way to achieve safety and to the emotionalization of political communication (particularly with regard to the effect of fear). In the twenty-first century, this type of effective risk governmentality seems prevalent in current digital cultures (see Boesel and Wiemer 2020), even though this notion of futures is of a paradoxical structure. As projections of the future that are based on probability, futures of risk are indebted to the past present; as a precaution, however, they view the future as something that will differ fundamentally from both the past and present.

Like futures of creation, futures of conservation demand decisions:

> It is not just a matter of preparedness and hazard pre-vention. This future type is essentially a normative project of defining and securing things worth preserving, for which the will and capacity to diverge from individual and generational concerns of the present is required. (Graf and Herzog 2016, 512)

Matters of distribution, for example, are central to these futures. Likewise, specific collective subjects and blueprints for action "arise" for these forms of subjects, insofar as the survival of the human species is involved (in keeping with apocalyptic futures of expectation). Here, the interrelationship between rhythms of time is significant as well, as these have to do with duration, maintenance, and reuse.

Preferable Futures—Envisioning, Projection and Negotiating Between Non-Knowledge and Action

As the above explanations have shown, envisioning, drafting, and negotiating futures is essentially impossible—and, at least under today's rationalities, the lyrics of Doris Day's signature song would seem to apply from a scientific perspective as well as from a more naive one: "Que sera, sera. Whatever will be, will be. The future's not ours to see."[15] Every projection of the future is a fiction, bordering on the sphere of non-knowledge to the extent that futures are unforeseeable and unpredictable, contingent,

15   Jay Livingston and Ray Evans, "Que Sera Sera (Whatever Will Be, Will Be)," 1956, sung by Doris Day, with Frank DeVol & His Orchestra, Columbia Records single # 4-40704.

and open. Likewise, every projection of the future is part of practice, to the extent that they are aimed at decisions, actions, and behaviors in the present and thus also contain exclusions and inclusions, and touch on questions of the (re-)distribution of power. Any projection of the future that demands little or no change in our present decisions, actions, and behaviors is not preferable in light of the fact that present meta-crises will probably worsen. Phantasms of the all-knowing and of exhaustive, planned control, on the other hand, have become obsolete, and the matter of the effect of our actions, intentions, and responsibilities in complex structures seem to disappear in cascades of operations (see the chapter by Nohr in this book). But to do nothing, to envision nothing, is not the answer. It bears repeating: if every projection of the future includes equal parts non-knowledge and practice, and as a result primarily generates knowledge and action, then envisioning, drafting, and negotiating preferable futures should reveal and reflect both the dual reference to the present day as well as their non-knowledge yet still practicing[16] while still being aware of their historical genealogies.

Against this backdrop, we observe different tiers, try to plumb the depths of our theoretical reflections, and develop different perspectives of possible, historical, and necessary negotiation zones.

---

16   The paradigm of transformative science (Schneidewind and Singer-Brodowski 2014) attempts to make this recursiveness productive from a methodological perspective (and is itself founded in the historical constellations of knowledge described above): system knowledge is acquired through an ongoing circular argument (analysis of the actual situation), target knowledge is developed (determination of the target situation) and various methods are employed to reduce the discrepancies between the two—through experiments, models, prototypes, and living labs. The acquired knowledge of transformation may then be used to accompany learning processes; it may also help detach experiences from the concrete situation and apply them to other contexts—thus changing the initial state, the system.

Saskia Hebert uses concrete "practice situations" from practical projects in the field of transformation design to outline three key skills, talents, or capacities of transformation design: sustain-ability, response-ability and prefer-ability. Sustainability, responsibility in the Harawayian sense of ability to respond, and the ability to prefer can help with viewing existing situations from different perspectives and transfering them to open, unknown, alternative futures by means of appropriate methodological interventions. The leap to a (fictional, imagined, simulated) future not only questions the present (and thus allows us to critique it in a different manner) but offers the opportunity to converge discourses, share perspectives and experiences and frame changed objectives in the here and now.

Wolfgang Jonas contextualizes his concept of transformation design in historical developments and newer design discourses. He illuminates the understanding of our world and society in current design research practice and questions its political relevance. With recourse to system-theoretical concepts, Jonas pleads for agonistic playgrounds in keeping with the strategy of Muddling Through, playgrounds that are aware of their boundaries in both senses of the word: as boundaries between a system and its surroundings in a system-theoretical sense and as the limitation of its validity and reach.

Based on the example of historical business simulations, Rolf F. Nohr analyzes a very specific interrelationship between playgrounds and futures that helps negotiate and rehearse a characteristically managerial rationality against the backdrop of increasing economic complexities. In doing so, Nohr demonstrates how a specific notion of the future is connected to formalized models, methods, and media technologies (board and computer games). The similarities (and differences) of prognostic visions of the future such as the *Limits to Growth* study, economic business simulations as rehearsal, and training and development scenarios demonstrate how reference to the future can create regimes of the closing of futures, especially in connection with media and specific epistemologies. Another thing that becomes clear is how actions in modeled or simulated spaces always strive to defuse the (threatening) contingency of the future. Planners (like the agent-operated simulation, the scenario) always aim to be teleologists, to tame contingencies.

Irina Kaldrack illuminates how more recent humanistic theories question existing epistemologies and, by taking new modes of perception and experience as a starting point, open up new ways of thinking to subsequently develop a new understanding of the world and appropriate political competences. Kaldrack outlines whether and how such theory-as-practice can be used for the benefit of transformative practice-as-theory.

As a whole, this volume is neither a complete project nor mere commentary: at its core, it is itself a "design," a suggestion, a vision of how we might view knowledge cultures and use them in our interdisciplinary work for the benefit of all. As an academic practice of thinking and writing, our book intersects directly with the described practices of prognostics, simulation and (planned and unplanned) changes in the world. We hope it encourages you to think about prefer-able futures as well as about the skills, talents, and experiences it will take to transform current prevalent cultures.

Translated by Emma Jane Stone

References

Amoore, Louise. 2013. *The Politics of Possibility: Risk and Security beyond Probability*. Durham, NC: Duke University Press.

Angerer, Marie Luise, and Naomie Gramlich, eds. 2020. *Feministisches Spekulieren: Genealogien, Narrationen, Zeitlichkeiten*. Berlin: Kadmos.

Angerer, Marie-Luise. 2017. *Ecology of Affect: Intensive Milieus and Contingent Encounters*. Lüneburg: meson press.

Aubin, David, and Amy Dahan Dalmedico. 2002. "Writing the History of Dynamical Systems and Chaos: Longue Durée and Revolution, Disciplines and Cultures." *Historia Mathematica* 29: 273–339.

Barad, Karen. 2007. *Meeting the Universe Halfway: Quantum Physics and the Entanglement of Matter and Meaning.* Durham, NC: Duke University Press.

Beck, Ulrich.1986. *Risikogesellschaft: Auf dem Weg in eine andere Moderne.* Frankfurt am Main: Suhrkamp.

Beer, Stafford.1962: *Kybernetik und Management.* Frankfurt am Main: Fischer.

Bennet, Jane. 2010. *Vibrant Matter: A Political Ecology of Things.* Durham, NC: Duke University Press.

Bertalanffy, Ludwig von. 1968. *General System Theory,* New York: Braziller.

Bösel, Bernd, and Wiemer, Serjoscha, eds. 2020. *Affective Transformations: Politics—Algorithms—Media.* Lüneburg: meson press.

Braidotti, Rosi. 2013. *The Posthuman.* Cambridge: Polity Press.

Carlowitz, Hans Carl von. 1713. *Sylvicultura Oeconomica, Oder Haußwirthliche Nachricht und Naturmäßige Anweisung Zur Wilden Baum-Zucht.* Leipzig: Braun.

Carson, Rachel. 1962. *Silent Spring.* Boston: Houghton Mifflin.

Conradi, Tobias, Heike Derwanz, and Florian Muhle, eds. 2013. *Strukturentstehung durch Verflechtung: Akteur-Netzwerk-Theorie(n) und Automatismen.* Paderborn: Fink.

Cubitt, Sean. 2017. *Finite Media: Environmental Implications of Digital Technologies.* Durham, NC: Duke University Press.

Desrosières, Alain. 1998. *The Politics of Large Numbers: History of Statistical Reasoning.* Cambridge, MA: Harvard University Press.

Forrester, Jay W. 1968. *Principles of Systems: Text and Workbook.* Cambridge, MA: Wright-Allen Press.

Gabrys, Jennifer. 2013. *Digital Rubbish: A Natural History of Electronics.* Michigan: The University of Michigan Press.

Graf, Rüdiger, and Benjamin Herzog. 2016. "Von der Geschichte der Zukunftsvorstellungen zur Geschichte ihrer Generierung". *Geschichte und Gesellschaft* 42: 497–515.

Haraway, Donna J. 2016. *Staying with the Trouble: Making Kin in the Chthulucene.* Durham, NC: Duke University Press.

Hörl, Erich. 2018. "Die environmentalitäre Situation." *Internationales Jahrbuch für Medienphilosophie* (4) 1: 221–50.

Horn, Eva. 2018. *The Future as Catastrophe: Imagining Disaster in the Modern Age.* New York: Columbia University Press.

Jonas, Wolfgang. 2014. "A Cybernetic Model of Design Research: Towards a Transdomain of Knowing." In *The Routledge Companion to Design Research,* edited by Paul A. Rodgers and Joyce Yee, 23–37. London: Taylor & Francis.

Jonas, Wolfgang. 2018. "Prolog/Prologue." In *Un/Certain Futures: Rollen des Designs in gesellschaftlichen Transformationsprozessen,* edited by Marius Förster, Saskia Hebert, Mona Hofmann, and Wolfgang Jonas, 16–21. Bielefeld: transcript.

Kahn, Hermann. 1970. *Ihr werdet es erleben: Voraussagen der Wissenschaft bis zum Jahr 2000.* München: Bertelsmann.

Kaldrack, Irina. 2011. *Imaginierte Wirksamkeit: Zwischen Performance und Bewegungserkennung.* Berlin: Kadmos.

26   Koselleck, Reinhard. 2004. *Futures Past: On the Semantics of Historical Time.* New York: Columbia University Press.

Leeker, Martina. 2020. "Speculate-as-speculate-can: Bedingungen von Spekulation als Kritik in digitalen Kulturen." In *Feministisches Spekulieren: Genealogien, Narrationen, Zeitlichkeiten,* edited by Marie Luise Angerer and Naomie Gramlich, 162–77. Berlin: Kadmos.

Leeker, Martina. 2021. "Pain, Befallen-ness, Conflict, Mediocrity: Dark Entanglements for Artistic Research and Critique in Digital Cultures." In *Throwing Gestures,* edited by Florian Bettel, Irina Kaldrack, and Konrad Strutz, 293–313. Wien: VfmK.

Leistert, Oliver, and Isabell Schrickel, eds. 2021. *Thinking the Problematic: Genealogies and Explorations between Philosophy and the Sciences.* Bielefeld: transcript.

Löffler, Petra. 2018. "Gaias Fortune: Kosmopolitik und Ökologie der Praktiken bei Latour und Stengers." In *Ökologien der Erde: Zur Wissensgeschichte und Aktualität der Gaia-Hypothese,* edited by Alexander Friedrich, Petra Löffler, and Niklas Schrape, 95–121. Lüneburg: meson press.

Neumann, John von. 1966. *Theory of Self-Reproducing Automata.* Edited by Arthur W. Burks. London: Urbana.

Nohr, Rolf F. 2019. *Unternehmensplanspiele 1955–1975: Die Herstellung unternehmerischer Rationalität im Spiel.* Münster: Lit.

Parikka, Jussi. 2015. *A Geology of Media.* Minneapolis: University of Minnesota Press

Pias, Claus. 2004. "Zeit der Kybernetik—Eine Einstimmung". In *Cybernetics—Kybernetik: The Macy Conferences 1946–1953. Essays and documents. Essays und Dokumente,* edited by Claus Pias, 9–42. Zürich: Diaphanes.

Rieger, Stefan. 2021. "Naive Physics: Gestures of Intuition." In *Throwing Gestures,* edited by Florian Bettel, Irina Kaldrack, and Konrad Strutz, 65–77. Wien: VfmK

Schneidewind, Uwe, and Mandy Singer-Brodowski. 2014. *Transformative Wissenschaft: Klimawandel im deutschen Wissenschafts- und Hochschulsystem.* Marburg: Metropolis.

Schrickel, Isabell. 2021. "The Problems of Modern Societies—Epistemic Design around 1970". In *Thinking the Problematic,* edited by Oliver Leistert and Isabell Schrickel, 35–68. Bielefeld: transcript.

Sprenger, Florian. 2019. *Epistemologien des Umgebens: Zur Geschichte, Ökologie und Biopolitik künstlicher Environments.* Bielefeld: transcript.

Taffel, Sy. 2019. *Digital Media Ecologies; Entanglements of Content, Code and Hardware.* New York: Bloomsbury Academic.

Ulam, Stanislaw. 1974. "Random Processes and Transformations." In *Stanislaw Ulam: Sets, Numbers, and Universes,* edited by William A. Beyer, Jan Mycielski, Gian-Carlo Rota, 326–37. Cambridge, MA: MIT Press.

Vehlken, Sebastian. 2014. "Das Atom-Ei des Columbus: Kernkraft und Computersimulation im Zeitalter der Hypothetizität." In *Trial and error: Szenarien medialen Handelns,* edited by Andreas Wolfsteiner and Markus Rautzenberg, 149–73. Paderborn: Fink.

PROBE-ABILITY

SUSTAIN-ABILITY

RESPONSE-ABILITY

PREFER-ABILITY

1

Designing Probe-ability: Time Machines and Other Useful Vehicles

Saskia Hebert

"Everyone designs who devises courses of action aimed at changing existing situations into preferred ones" (Simon [1969] 1996, 111). Simon's well-known statement raises a number of questions. First, what would constitute "preferred" situations (why, when, and for whom), and secondly, what is the "existing" situation—and how would "devising courses of action" relate to actual, concrete change. In the following discussion, I unfold how transformation design (as a discipline) can deliver aesthetic, sense-able narratives, simulations, and environments that can lead to different perceptions, experiences, and expectations of our common future. Designing processes, situative prototypes, information and

systems requires specific talents and abilities that can be trained. While the classic roles of "designer," "consumer," "critic," and "public" are constantly interchanging and even dissolving, we need to re-think and re-member where we came from—and still design, build, and test alternative ways to perceive what is called "reality" or predictions of "the future." In other words, we urgently need to enhance our ability to "probe" (im)probable futures.

Interviewer: "What are the boundaries of Design?"
Charles Eames: "What are the boundaries of problems?"
—Eames 1972, 0:00:55

Unfolding the Map: A Foggy Localization

The relatively young discipline of transformation design has a lot on its plate. The world is rapidly transforming and so few of the changes offer confidence that conditions will be better, more just, or sustainable. Futures close in and open up on an almost weekly basis. Since preliminary work on this essay first began four years ago, the US government pulled out of Paris Agreement and then re-joined it again, yet there are still governments and individuals denying that there is any human influence on climate change. On the other hand, new voices made themselves heard. Only weeks before the authors of this publication met at the DCRL conference in September 2018, a Swedish teen decided to boycott her classes on Fridays to "school strike for climate" and, soon after, her protest went viral. It morphed into the global movement known today as Fridays for Future, popularizing the demand for a livable future for the upcoming generation.

Obviously, even these digital natives have little faith that the ongoing digital revolution will be a solution. In spite of the invention of ever more apps and algorithms, artificial intelligence (AI) and vast data collections, the future has not become more controllable or predictable over the last fifty years. Climate change and digitalization are just two developments among many that are contributing to increasing feelings of insecurity and the loss of improving prospects in terms of wealth, security, and happiness. As a result, "the future is not what it used to be." Today, in significant contrast to preceding generations, many people in the developed Western world believe that their children will not be better off than themselves.[1] But how is this related to design, if at all? I argue that if the present transformation leaves no stone unturned, the same is also true for the discipline of design. Like Wolfgang Jonas (as he states in his contribution to this volume) I am convinced that in stark contrast to the reassuring conviction expressed in the statement by Charles Eames reprinted above, design as a means of problem-solving, an approach familiar to engineers, is no longer fit for purpose— especially not when the problems to be solved reach the systemic, societal, and cultural dimensions of those we are currently witnessing. Nevertheless, the discipline of design still offers some useful tools and talents that can and should be integrated in a joint effort to open up futures again.[2] Although designers

1   One example of this idea being expressed is when it is noted by a character (representing Hans Joachim Schellnhuber) in the graphic novel published by the WBGU to accompany their "Great Transformation" Report from 2011 (Hamann et al. 2014, 21). On the uncertainty of futures, see also Förster et al. 2018.

2   Achieving such an opening up would mean dropping two key approaches: first, design-as-solutionism, which (often unintentionally) contributes to existing problems or creates new ones, and second, design-as-artform, where ideas are attached to individual creators (authors) and are as often

within industrialized societies arguably cannot solve the issues mentioned above with the same kind of thinking that was used while the problems were being created, it seems useful to integrate some of the well-known tools and talents the discipline offers into the context of *different thinking*—for example, in order to develop alternative ideas and approaches towards *future imaginaries* beyond a planned and predicted, ever prolonged present. Design can speculate and project and is also able to pro-totype, to make ideas visible, perceivable, and experienceable, which allows others to join in, to test and discuss what could be valid alternative options. That is what I call "probe-ability"—very different from probability as a measure of (un)certainty con-cerning future events and developments.

To elaborate, in the following section I suggest alternative per-spectives and describe three example projects from Master of Arts in Transformation Design students at Braunschweig Univer-sity of Art (HBK). Finally, there will be a non-clusion instead of a conclusion: to use a metaphor cited by Wolfgang Jonas, muddling through swampy lowlands is a never-ending process, only partly enabling people engaged in it to step back and reflect—and to orientate.

What Transformation? Increasing Uncertainties and Normative Concepts

The title of Braunschweig's Master of Transformation Design is a reference to the concept of a *Great Transformation* described by members of the German Advisory Council on Global Change in their 2011 flagship report (WBGU 2011).[3] They argued that any

as not sold off to the highest bidder or, indeed, any client who can afford to pay.

3   The WBGU referred to Karl Polanyi's groundbreaking analysis of the same title, which described how markets were being untethered from their societal benefit (Polanyi 1945) during industrialization, and how societies (and individuals) had to adapt—and respectively failed (Polanyi 1945).

transformation has to be directed towards sustainability and social justice (WBGU 2011), proposing a normative concept of eco-social cultural change. Although not linked to any party's program, such positions are deeply political—and sound disturbing to members of the global economic elite and others.[4] If humankind could finally accept that there are "limits to growth" (Meadows et al. 1972) and, at the same time, would challenge the idea of a "green economy" merely decoupling the further rise of global wealth from the further rise of global resource depletion, almost all our values, everything that we are taught at school and hear on a daily basis would be thrown into question. If "growth" (the mantra so frequently found alongside "wealth" and "development") were no longer a good thing per se, economic logic and personal decisions would have to be re-evaluated. Literally everything from food, travel, family, work, politics, and international relations would be turned upside down. It is an especially challenging thought-experiment given transformations at such scale are rarely smooth, but resembling instead a chaotic, bumpy ride, desynchronizing lifeworlds at different speeds and scales while value systems and beliefs reorganize. Both personal and institutional levels of experienced uncertainty and perceived insecurity—with the resulting fear of losing privileges or basic security fueling conflicts across the world and fostering "cognitive dissonance," first described by Leon Festinger in 1957 (Festinger 1957). Supported by the new media, people build up their own "realities" based on "alternative facts"—while public discourse is discredited and mistrusted even in countries that guarantee free speech. In that respect, it does not help at all that the requested transformational change comes with a very unpopular if not frightening vocabulary containing terms such as *relinquishment, retreat,* and *reduction.*

4   Interestingly enough, the council's members understand that a cultural shift is necessary despite the majority being rooted in the natural sciences. They call for a new "societal contract," comprising the just depletion of resources, an end to the exploitation of the earth's treasures and fair access to goods (and services) around the globe.

What Design? (Un)Happily Muddling Through

It is not only language that hinders any necessary adaptation. Cultural paradigms and deeply rooted beliefs evolve much more slowly than scientific findings, as we can see during the ongoing pandemic, for example. In Western civilizations there is still a very strong belief that "progress" and "technical development" will help us to "innovate" and improve literally everything, to find solutions for existing problems, to "make the world a better place," as Google, Facebook, and other Silicon Valley companies claim. At the same time, it has become quite obvious that all the fantastic things invented previously (such as the steam engine, electricity, petro-chemical products, and the internet) have contributed to enormous and unprecedented wealth, but also to the instigation of a catastrophic development that threatens all people, no matter how much money they have—although, of course, being rich can buy a lot of risk reduction.

While many people believe, or pretend to believe, that transformative "change by design" is still possible, others are convinced that "change by disaster" is imminent[5]—or already happening right now in front of our eyes. From a design perspective, the biggest problem is not the disagreement between those two groups (even if climate change deniers have done everything to put us all at even more risk), but that both views prevent any real change action. Neither the optimist (who believes in techno-fixes, delivered in a timely fashion by smart designers) nor the pessimist (who believes there is nothing to be done to fix things at all) is likely to transform anything, or to practice "the arts of living on a damaged planet," as Anna Tsing (2017) puts it.[6] But what can

5   For the design/disaster discussion see also Welzer and Sommer (2014) or the annual design conference organized by the M.A. in Eco-Social Design program at the Free University of Bozen-Bolzano.

6   The economist and former head of the Wuppertal Institute, Uwe Schneidewind, arrives at a similar term he calls "Future Art" (in German: *Zukunftskunst*, Schneidewind 2018)—although his concept of "Art" seems rather limited here.

design, itself an insecure and unsettled discipline, contribute
here? What possibilities are there, for example, to leave the probable paths of institutional, systemic, and mental infrastructures of ever-new inventions, products, fashion trends, and sales strategies? To cite Victor Papanek's famous (self)critique:

> There are professions more harmful than industrial design, but only a very few of them. And possibly only one profession is phonier. Advertising design, in persuading people to buy things they don't need, with money they don't have, in order to impress others who don't care, is probably the phoniest field in existence today. (Papanek 1985, 9)

How can designers (happily!) "muddle through"[7] to develop and depict livable *future imaginaries*? Moreover, if they knew how, should they really do it—after all that has gone wrong with collective dreams and visions in the past? Wouldn't they support the current system instead of changing it in the end? And if they finally did: Who would they have as clients? Who would pay their bills?

There are no simple answers to these serious questions. But, as a trained architect, I agree with Jonas's understanding of design as a *projection*, in German *Entwerfen*, literally throwing something (*werfen*) from a point (*ent-*) to an unknown condition. Projecting or layering different (or preferred) situations in contrast to existing ones, as Herbert Simon's ([1969] 1996) famous design definition suggests, can open up unconventional, unexpected, and unlikely trajectories, engage joint discussions, and mobilize collective energies. The beauty of the "muddling," in this case, lies in the careful calibration of *knowns* and *unknowns*. For example, any local knowledge can be very valuable for any design process—just as much as outside expertise can be helpful and valuable in going beyond the ordinary, the expected, and the likely.

---

7 See "Happily Muddling Through" by Wolfgang Jonas in this book.

"Design as *ent/werfen*" means to *imagine*—through conceptual or scenario work, model making, storytelling, performing, in cooperation, by chance or by choice. The outcomes of these imaginative processes are rarely products or artefacts in the old "design" sense—as demonstrated by the examples below. With reference to these three projects, I will elaborate on my understanding of *probe-ability*—the ability to experiment with, test, and experience cores, frames, and concepts of alternative, different, maybe sustainable possible futures.

No Futures? Designing for Discourse

I have not yet discussed the term "futures," used mainly in the plural here. The future (singular) is a place no one has ever been, so it lacks scientific evidence and slips away from any attempt to install a true/false dichotomy. But, undisputedly, the future follows the present, which means that to some extent things (or people, habits, values) will continue to exist, at least for a certain timeframe. Within that future time space, some things (or rhythms, or events) are more likely to keep occurring than others: the probability of day and night, for example, is pretty high, while that of iPods is not. The thing is, it is impossible to *know* because the future is "unavailable" as Hartmut Rosa (2018) puts it.[8] But of course our present actions can open up (or hinder) future developments—and non-action, too, contributes to "designing" futures. Just going on with business as usual, for example, has become not just questionable but irresponsible under the circumstances described above. Jared Diamond (2011) warns us that a

8   The title of sociologist Hartmut Rosa's book, *Unverfügbarkeit*, has been translated as *The Uncontrollability of The World*, which is quite different to the literal translation, "Unavailability," concerning the opportunity to "design (a) future." In his book, Rosa explains aspects of his larger work, resonance theory, in their dilemmatic and conflicting qualities. Rosa claims that the modern habit of extending control, of bringing things "into reach" (German: *Reichweite*) sometimes disturbs and distorts the weak relation humans have towards their given world even further.

common feature of failing societies is the tendency to intensify **37**
their (unhealthy, unsustainable) patterns—because they don't
know better and can't think clearly under stress.[9]

In his article "Farewell Utopia?"[10] Ernst Bloch refers to exactly the
same phenomenon when he differentiates between "false" and
"real" future (German: *"falsche" oder "echte Zukunft"*), referring to
the amount of contingent or just (im)probable things that could
happen in the "mighty sphere of the not-yet" (1980,108). According
to him, it is a sign of a false (or simply non-human) future if there
are too few options for how things could happen. In that sense,
the repetitive "feedback-looped present" that Rolf F. Nohr and
Irina Kaldrack describe in the introduction to this volume is false
precisely because of its claimed predictive precision.

So, the future closes in on us, becomes inevitable, brings "change
by disaster" or at least degenerates to an "unreal" future in the
sense described by Ernst Bloch. Let's stay there for a moment
and look at the different unpleasant possibilities, using the well-
known graphics of a (modified) future or scenario cone as it is
used in strategic foresight and other futurologist methodologies
(fig. 1). The cone revolves around a horizontal axis (= time), starts
now (= zero) and opens up towards a future (= x) that ranges (on
the y-axis) from the edges of unlikeliness towards the center and
depicts possible, plausible, and probable fields of development.
Within that shape lies a smaller cone depicting a preferable
future—or, in other words, the future we want to achieve.

If we take natural science and climate research seriously,[11] this
overlap depicts not much more than a friendly self-deception.

---

9   Social psychologist Harald Welzer summarizes Diamond's example of the
      Greenland Vikings who, at a time of scarce food resources, would not eat
      fish because for them, it was not proper food—a deadly lack of flexibility
      concerning their diet (Welzer 2014,15).

10   In German: *Abschied von der Utopie*, Bloch 1980.

11   See, for example (IPCC 2014) and other reports of the Intergovern-
      mental Panel on Climate Change (IPCC); https://www.ipcc.ch/report/
      sixth-assessment-report-cycle/.

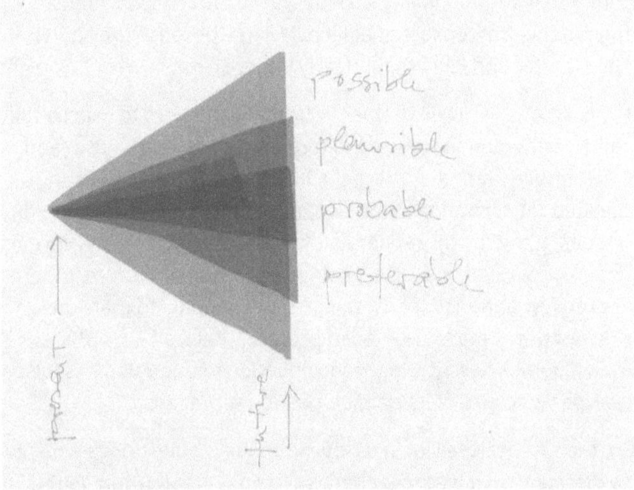

[Fig. 1] Classical future / scenario cone graphic: the (brown) field of preferable development lies well within the (blue) field of the possible, the plausible, and the probable (own adaptation).

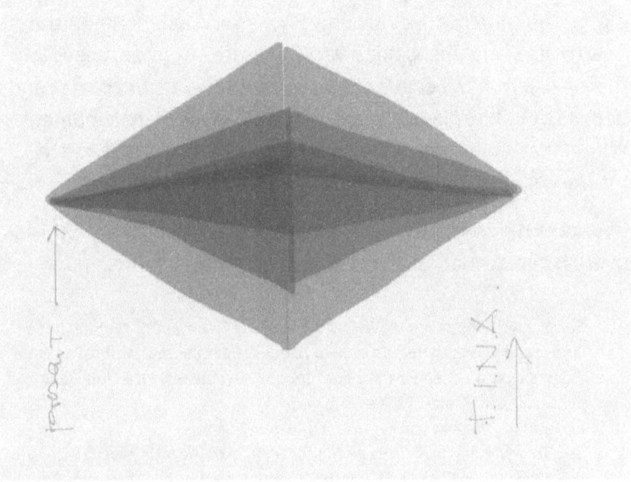

[Fig. 2] The T.I.N.A. scenario cone: closed future, no choice.

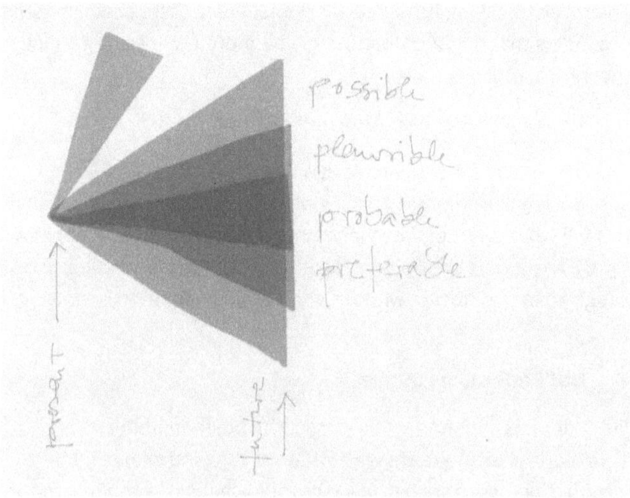

[Fig. 3] The NPF scenario cone: the preferable is not available.

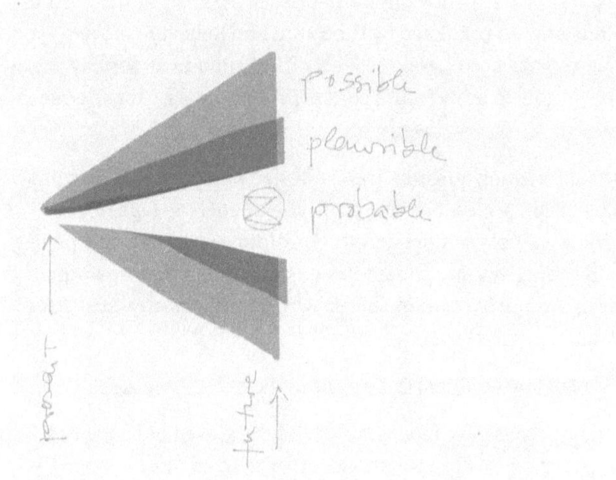

[Fig. 4] The FWU scenario cone: human futures are no longer available.

 The three following future cones depict more or less catastrophic prospects that might unfortunately be more accurate regarding the information we have.

T.I.N.A. (There Is No Alternative)

There is just one way to arrive at a (human) future at all—the suspension of democracy for a global "eco-dictatorship" in order to save what is left of Earth (and limiting global warming to below 1.5°C). A future is possible (or, as Rosa would say, available), but at a high cost: it is closed, without choice, alternative or escape (fig. 2).

Not Preferable Futures

Fig. 3 depicts something still worse: the position of the "preferable" cone is incongruent with what we can (and will) get. There is a future, but it is not anything we would choose—probably this is what will happen if we go on as we are.

Future Without Us

Fig. 4 shows a slightly different (or escalated) version of the previous one: As predicted by the Extinction Rebellion movement, the "6th mass extinction" collects its toll and excludes any species that is able to draw future cones from the game; humans become extinct.

The interesting question from a design perspective is how possible, even preferable futures can be opened up (again). How radical, critical and presumptuous or how empathic, compelling, and seductive can / should designs be? Where do transformation designers position themselves, who do they collaborate with and what are their respective roles?

Future-Abilities: Capacity Building

If being a designer means "to devise courses of action aimed at changing existing situations into preferred ones" (Simon [1969] 1996), there is yet another sense in which this definition

is interesting that has not previously been discussed. Firstly,
Simon expands the job definition significantly: both Greta Thunberg and Donald Trump, just to mention two very different but well-known people, could call themselves *designers*, if what they are aiming for seems preferred to *them*. Secondly, that example in particular would cause legitimate concerns. Transformation designers, it seems, would have to make sure that they don't just serve their own interest (or the interests of a single client, or a small group they belong to), but that their definition of the "preferred" is approved in a wider sense. While Greta Thunberg's goals might align with a whole generation's idea of a sustainable world, Trump's America-first policy would not meet the same standards, being neither inclusive nor sustainable. It seems crucial to develop a protocol to define what is "preferred," and to disclose honestly by whom, how, and under which conditions that definition would be agreed on.

Regarding the context referred to in this text, these "preferred" situations would at least have to be described according to their sustainability (how they would preserve resources for future generations) and their accessibility (who they would include or exclude). Both aspects, by the way, reflect what lies at the core of the sustainable development definition coined at the Brundtland commission in 1987 (Hauff 1987): the question of inter- and intragenerational justice. However, it not only has to be asked what "preferred" (why, when and for whom) would mean, but what currently "exists." The "arts of living on a damaged planet" (Tsing 2017) therefore demand certain talents, competencies, and capacities—or, as I like to put it, future-abilities. I call those talents *sustain-, response- and prefer-ability*:

Sustain-ability means the ability to preserve inherited structures, knowledge treasures, and skills—and to work with them instead of starting over again and again, wasting valuable resources. Sometimes though, keeping things as they are demands huge effort: life transforms everything continuously over time, and "not keeping pace with change" contains a risk of being left behind or losing your social network. In the context of the design discipline—whether we consider object design, social design, or any other design—*sustain-ability* has always been crucial. Not wasting resources, designing with what is (regionally) at hand and the question of durability (especially for products) are very obvious examples of how precaution (German: *Vorsorge*) always played a part in decision-making—at least before the apparent availability of everything, everywhere, instantly.

Response-ability is a term Donna Haraway coined (e.g., Haraway 2016).[12] It (literally) describes the will to take responsibility, but also to join in with an interdisciplinary, interspecies discourse, listening and answering—responding—with care. Response-ability is needed in all forms of multivocal decision making, including the ability to take the standpoint and perspective of other people (or species). Seeing situations through the eyes of another is as close as we can get to diverse encounters—and possible compromises deriving from that. This awareness of and respect for the other of course includes the designerly question of clientship. It is not always the person with the money that we're designing for, we're designing for the people who are going to use what we've created. And although it is not at all trivial to include those people in the design process, there are methods and ways of participatory and open or even co-design that help to integrate multiple perspectives.

Last but not least, *prefer-ability*, meaning the capacity to prefer, to dream, to balance the seemingly impossible and the given (or, as Musil (1994) puts it, a "sense of reality" with the "sense of possibility"), lies at the core of what design can contribute to

12 Haraway uses the term both in a descriptive and in a normative sense. In her contribution to Anna Tsing's book, *Arts of Living on a Damaged Planet* (2017), she mentions a "feminist ethic of 'response-ability'" (Haraway 2017, M32) and describes a "capacity to respond" (M38). In her book, *Staying with the Trouble* (Haraway 2016), response-ability is frequently used to specify the sympoietic, non-hierarchical relationships between different species and worlds that (might) create worlds other than those we know today.

a response-able discourse about sustain-able futures. A valid criticism of current conditions does not imply valid proposals for alternative modes and models of existence. It is never easy to imagine what does not exist, what nobody knows, and where nobody has ever been: the work of designing (as *ent-werfen*) and its testing in probes and prototypes enhances the probe-ability needed to peek into that future—and to increase the probability of opening up different options instead of closing them.

To do this, design can use many well-known (and some less known) tools—or invent new ones. Some of those tools will be introduced in the following examples from the master's program at HBK Braunschweig and linked to the capacities mentioned above.

Time Machines and Other Useful Vehicles: Probe-able Prototyping

The following examples are the results of three projects conducted at HBK Braunschweig. Students were given a thematic direction, formed groups, and cooperated with external partners, to create the form and content of their contribution over the course of one semester. The result was either a joint presentation (as in the first example), individual projects (like the second example) or something in-between (as in the third). To keep the descriptions short and sharp, the project design credits, partners, and participants are listed in the footnotes.[13]

Sustain-ability: UN/REAL ESTATES

The questions posed in the UN/REAL ESTATES project were first, how a former concrete factory in Stolpe, a village in rural Brandenburg, could be transformed into a "culture and business park"—and second, who, apart from the owner, would have to

13   Additional information on the projects can be found at: www.transform-azine.de

44　be involved.[14] Since the site had been specialized (fabricating concrete segments) and was clearly no longer operational (no more concrete segments would ever be fabricated), the question of sustain-ability was crucial. How could the atmosphere, the location on the Oder River, the new owners, or elements of its former function (along with a lot of very stable concrete) become part of its future existence?

Students visited the site twice. They started their analysis with the past, collecting samples from the site, arranging and re-using them in a workshop we called *Speculative Forensics*. During the workshop, their perspective changed from what-was-there to what-could-be. Traces of the past were integrated into small installations and short stories that opened up new horizons in both space and time. Based on those first impressions, the teams worked in six groups, coming back for a second workshop during which all future visions had to be simulated—in settings I like to call *Time Machines*, because the audience (people from Stolpe, officials, and friends of the owners) were able to take part in a situation that was and was not there, testing the probe-ability in a situation of *collective fiction*.

For example, all guests co-created and witnessed the founding ceremony of a non-profit organization that was established to develop and run the site. All visitors were also later involved in a cross-cultural kitchen run by a diversity project and had the opportunity to visit a workshop for re-skilling and combining old crafts with new habits. Afterwards, everyone met up at an on-site pop-up bar and all suggestions were discussed.

14　This project seminar was a cooperation between site owner Uli Kaiser of Kulturpark Stolpe GmbH and Anke Strauss from the Department of Organizational Theory, European University Viadrina Frankfurt (Oder). The following Braunschweig students participated: Pedro Botelho Faim, Catherine Sydow, Hui Tang, Liwei Liu, Bingru Yu, and Marieke Guder. Artist Diana Lucas-Drogan and performer Christina Ciupke took part in workshops on site.

For "UN/MAKING HEIMAT," a course held in 2019,[15] two students decided to tackle the question of how the shifting discourses of the far right "unmake" what we perceive as our *Heimat* (homeland)—by, for example, introducing new vocabulary, derogatory discussion styles, self-victimization (by complaining about the alleged decline of free speech), and scaring others by threatening them both physically and psychologically.

They departed from their own lived experience, describing situations where they involuntarily witnessed or had been the target of verbal hostility, and found it very challenging to adequately react and take a stance against it. They researched why it is so difficult for the (silent) majority to come forward and object or "speak up" (hence the title of the project, *Gegenreden*—Objections) aggressors, and learned about, for example, the insecurities of being exposed to a public when you can't be sure which side they are on, and the complexities of confronting people, whether it's a member of the family disagreeing, a stranger looking for trouble, or someone willing to use violence.

The students worked on the question of how to develop designerly positions within this vast problem space. In the end, they decided to conceptualize a "wall newspaper" (German: *Wandzeitung)* consisting of A4 sheets, that could be printed by anyone who wanted to support the project or join the regular workshops and roundtables that served as "editorial meetings" and an online platform.[16] The wall newspaper featured different categories of article including readers' letters telling of their own experiences in critical situations (sometimes describing how they managed to speak up, sometimes how they failed to do so), and essays by people working in such contexts offering advice and useful information.

15　*Gegenreden* was authored by Jakob Hubmann and Veronika Schneider during a semester course I ran with my colleague, Dr. Andreas Unteidig, in 2019.

16　www.gegenreden.de, accessed March 5, 2022.

In their reflection, the students reported that they, at times, were overwhelmed by the heaviness of their chosen subject—and that following the transformation design-mantra of leaving their comfort zone and "going to where it hurts" did indeed cause them real pain. On the other hand, the feedback they got (and the reputation, including an invitation to present at the 2019 DGTF conference) showed how important such approaches are—and how relevant it is to take on response-ability in every sense.

Prefer-ability: IM/MOBILE CULTURES

In this third example, a project called IM/MOBILE CULTURES,[17] three teams of students were assigned an almost unsolvable task: to develop scenarios for a post-fossil-fuel future world in Salzgitter, a city which depends heavily on cars and the automotive industry. The students went through a scenario-building process that began with a field trip. From there, they developed some extreme raw scenarios and ended up with three back-casting stories, looking back from a point in the future and describing how they got there.

The first team explored the generation gap by inventing a future teenager, Emma, whose homework assignment is to analyze the transport culture of the near past (which is, of course, our present). By interviewing fictional experts, Emma learns many things that surprise or shock her: The amount of car accidents, air pollution, traffic noise, the high number of private cars, and the existence of human-driven buses that run on a fixed schedule. In her world, almost everything seems to have changed, including transport: housing, work, leisure and family concepts, and attitudes towards nature and ecology.

17   The IM/MOBILE CULTURES project took place in 2016/17 and was held in cooperation with the Department of Environment and City Development of the City of Salzgitter, a dispersed town of 100,000 inhabitants southeast of Braunschweig. Project participants were Mia Braun, Leon Brintrup, Anna Bruhl, Arved Bünning, Pedro Faim, Marius Förster, Marieke Guder, Maik Hauck, Mona Hofmann, Liwei Liu, Felix Pliester, Catherine Sydow, Hui Tang, and Bingru Yu.

The second team kept closer to our present reality, replacing cars with bikes. By converting the slogan "Copenhagenize" into "Salzgitterize" they imagined a future where the city is no longer known primarily for car manufacturing, but for its clever implementation of an ambitious bike-riding and -sharing concept. The story is told by a fictional member of the local authorities who, in 2042, makes a presentation to other city officials who want to learn from Salzgitter—a humorous and tempting prospect for the project's partners.

The third team was interested in Salzgitter's fertile soil, something they had seen and heard about in stories. They imagined a process that started with a festival for people interested in alternative ways of living. In their story, a group of eco-activists meet and decide to buy a farm, converting the land to *Kulturland* (cultivated land and, literally, land of culture) according to the principles of permaculture. The collective thrives and survives every crisis including a loss of EU funding, new plant diseases arriving with a changing climate, and peak phosphorous. In the end, Salzgitter becomes successful once again, but in a way that nobody from there would have (or could have) imagined.

Ultimately, we were able to present the stories to the city council's building and environment board. The board members were happy to have been presented with three different and, despite all critique, positive versions of Salzgitter's future. It was particularly helpful to them. As residents of a city facing deindustrialization, poverty, and segregation, they seemed to have lost their *prefer-ability*. The future, they told us, had become a burdensome, unpleasant subject in an unpromising area in which no fame (and no voters) were to be gained.

Nonclusion

Of course, these short descriptions (severely lacking the images that were produced to support them) do not "solve" any of the huge questions posed above, nor do they represent or claim any universality. Also, they must not be read as recipes: use this, avoid that, heat, and wait for a certain time.

Another finding was that the academic framing of the projects offered both advantages and difficulties. The opportunity to think "outside the box" without any economic interests or clients, and the opportunity to create trustful environments for "unruly" or rough thinking was very helpful, while the agency of the students often remained unclear. During the semester, they had difficulties finding their individual positions and interests in the vast fields of investigation, and afterwards they had to continue with other courses so were unable to take their (sometimes very promising) ideas further. Additionally, the project's partners seemed to have difficulties relating to the outcome. In Stolpe, our feeling was that the "gift" we had brought was not properly appreciated (perhaps because of its gift status), in Salzgitter we even frightened some members of the authorities, and for *Gegenreden* there was no pre-cast "client" or partner at all, so in the end no one took the project further.

Nevertheless, these experiments, simulating (or prototyping) alternative environments and decision-making structures or agencies, seem to be good examples of how institutions (such as universities) would have to adapt in the current state of crisis (or catastrophe). A cultural shift requires skills, talents, and capacities that are not necessarily available or transmittable in a hierarchical education system where older people teach younger people based on their experience.

Instead, I like to think of education and research as a horizontal, unruly, and rippled structure that enables trust and experi-ence—apart from grades and careers. A shift in the design dis-cipline is needed: from the design of objects or services (or the illusion of control) to the possible subjects of a design that has open methods and at the same time is committed towards the normative target of future-ability. Design, and also architecture, art, and similar disciplines have a special role in a field that

requires integration into transdisciplinary collaboration and new 49
forms of assignments. They can help develop concepts, ideas, and images of alternative futures, *future imaginaries*, and even test them in prototypical and probe-able situations.[18] This, of course, should not be conceived as a privilege, but rather as a duty: to enable oneself (and others) to engage in long, hard, and sometimes conflicted processes without losing a sense of humor, joy, and self-respect. In other words, to train, try, and probe our personal and collective *sustain-, response-* and *prefer-abilities*.

References

Bloch, Ernst, and Hanna Gekle. 1980. *Abschied von der Utopie? Vorträge.* Edition Suhrkamp, 1st ed. Frankfurt am Main: Suhrkamp.

Diamond, Jared M. 2011. *Collapse: How Societies Choose to Fail or Succeed.* New York: Penguin Books.

Eames, Charles. 1972. "What Are the Boundaries of Problems?" Interview at the Musée des Arts Décoratifs, Palais de Louvre. Accessed March 5, 2022. https://www.youtube.com/watch?v=3xYi2rd1QCg.

Festinger, Leon. 1957. *A Theory of Cognitive Dissonance.* Stanford: Stanford University Press.

Förster, Marius, Saskia Hebert, Mona Hofmann, and Wolfgang Jonas, eds. 2018. *Un/Certain Futures: Rollen des Designs in gesellschaftlichen Transformationsprozessen.* Bielefeld: Transcript.

Hamann, Alexandra, Claudia Zea-Schmidt, and Reinhold Leinfelder, eds. 2014. *The Great Transformation: Climate—Can We Beat the Heat?* Translated by Bob Culverhouse. Berlin: German Advisory Council on Global Change (WBGU).

Haraway, Donna J. 2016. *Staying with the Trouble: Making Kin in the Chthulucene.* Durham, NC: Duke University Press.

Haraway, Donna J. 2017. "Symbiogenesis, Sympoiesis, and Art Science Activisms for Staying with the Trouble." In *Arts of Living on a Damaged Planet*, edited by Anna L. Tsing, Heather Anne Swanson, Elaine Gan, and Nils Bubandt, M25–M50. Minneapolis: University of Minnesota Press.

Hauff, Volker, ed. 1987. *Unsere gemeinsame Zukunft: Der Brundtland-Bericht der Weltkommission für Umwelt und Entwicklung.* Greven: Eggenkamp Verlag.

Hebert, Saskia, and Thomas Malorny. 2019. "Perforierte Wirklichkeit und mögliche Zukünfte: Ein Gespräch." In *Komplement und Verstärker: Zum Verhältnis von Stadtplanung, künstlerischen Praktiken und Kulturinstitutionen*, edited by Isabel Maria

18   See also: Hebert and Malorny (2019).

50   Finkenberger, Eva-Maria Baumeister, and Christian Koch, 108–21. Berlin: jovis Verlag.

IPCC. 2014. *Climate Change 2014: Synthesis Report. Contribution of Working Groups I, II and III to the Fifth Assessment Report of the Intergovernmental Panel on Climate Change.* [Core Writing Team, R.K. Pachauri and L.A. Meyer (eds.)]. Geneva: IPCC.

Meadows, Donella, Dennis Meadows, Jørgen Randers, and William W. Behrens III. 1972. *Die Grenzen des Wachstums: Bericht des Club of Rome zur Lage der Menschheit.* Aus dem Amerikanischen von Hans-Dieter Heck. Stuttgart: Deutsche Verlags-Anstalt.

Musil, Robert. 1994. *Der Mann ohne Eigenschaften.* Reinbek: Rowohlt Taschenbuch Verlag.

Papanek, Victor. 1985. *Design for the Real World: Human Ecology and Social Change.* 2nd ed. London: Thames & Hudson.

Rosa, Hartmut. 2018. *Unverfügbarkeit, Unruhe bewahren.* Wien: Residenz Verlag.

Rosa, Hartmut. 2020. *The Uncontrollability of the World.* Cambridge, UK: Polity Press.

Schneidewind, Uwe. 2018. *Die große Transformation: Eine Einführung in die Kunst gesellschaftlichen Wandels.* Frankfurt am Main: Fischer Taschenbuch.

Simon, Herbert A. (1969) 1996. *The Sciences of the Artificial.* 3rd ed. Cambridge, MA: MIT Press.

Thiery, W. et al. 2021. "Intergenerational Inequities in Exposure to Climate Extremes." *Science* 374 (6564): 15860. DOI: 10.1126/science.abi7339.

Tsing, Anna L., Heather Anne Swanson, Elaine Gan, and Nils Bubandt, eds. 2017. *Arts of Living on a Damaged Planet: Ghosts of the Anthropocene.* Minneapolis: University of Minnesota Press.

WBGU—German Advisory Council on Global Change, ed. 2011: *World in Transition: A Social Contract for Sustainability.* Flagship Report. Berlin: WBGU.

Welzer, Harald. 2014. *Selbst denken: Eine Anleitung zum Widerstand.* 8th ed. Frankfurt am Main: Fischer Taschenbuch.

Welzer, Harald, and Bernd Sommer. 2014. *Transformationsdesign: Wege in eine zukunftsfähige Moderne.* Munich: Oekom Verlag.

TRANSFORMATIVE DESIGN

PREDICTION

PROJECTION

MUDDLING THROUGH

MORALITY

SERENITY

PLAYFULNESS

2

Happily Muddling Through: Potentials and Limits of Transformative Design Approaches

Wolfgang Jonas

One of the myths adopted from the "hard" sciences was the idea that the future is predictable. Future states of *trivial machines* might be predictable, but socio-technical-cultural systems are *nontrivial machines* that are irreversible in time. Their development is evolutionary; explanations can only be delivered post-hoc. Not even the most comprehensive data resources with the most "intelligent" algorithms would be able to produce a *Laplacean Demon*. Abraham Lincoln is quoted as saying that "the best way to predict the future is to create it." So, we depend on *the design way:* we create options, futures in stock, in order not to be taken by surprise too much, the results of which are both

promising (see emancipatory endeavours such as social design and transformation design) and disappointing (see manipulative designs like *Cambridge Analytica*, *Facebook* or the *Trump* campaign). The focus of this essay is on the potentials and limits of the former, promising approaches of social / transformative design with an argument for more theoretical reflection and professional serenity.

There is no purer myth than the notion of a science which has been purged of all myth.
—Michel Serres

Initial Considerations and Questions

This text is intended to be a discussion piece in the context of the emerging field of transformative design theories, methodologies, and practices such as transformation design, transition design, social design, etc.[1] "Un/certain futures" is a perennial topic in the MA in Transformation Design,[2] a program that has been running successfully at Braunschweig University of Art since 2015. The inspiration for this reflective piece was the experience of working on an anthology, *Un/Certain Futures—Rollen des Designs in gesellschaftlichen Transformationsprozessen* (The Role of Design in Social Transformation Processes) (Förster et al. 2018). Some of the

---

1   A shorter version was published in the Journal of Design Thinking, University of Tehran, 2020: https://jdt.ut.ac.ir

2   See https://www.hbk-bs.de/studium/studienangebot/transformation-design/ and http://transformazine.de/. See also Jonas et al. (2016).

questions that arose included: Can futures be designed for the 55
better in a sustainable way? Will the effects of well-intentioned
creative design— interventions in otherwise independently
evolving autopoietic systems[3]—always be internally determined
reactions that appear random to external observers? Do we have
consensus on what the "better" that we are aspiring to actually
is? Who is "we" in this context? Is it possible that design is far too
naïve in assessing its potential to exert political influence? Should
even the concept of design perhaps be completely reconsidered?

Heinz von Förster (1995, np) argued that in a culture open to
learning the only legitimate questions are those that cannot be
decided. So, we cannot expect definite answers to these big questions; we should even be skeptical if anyone claims to be able to
provide them. But we can expect lots of preliminary, crazy, and
contradictory answers that might contribute to a more comprehensive—albeit fuzzy and dynamic—picture of the new field of
transformative design.

Calculation or Design: Prediction or Projection?

The idea that the future is predictable, a matter of calculation,
was a scientific myth adopted from the "hard" sciences; an
expectation that was also suggested—at least implicitly—in the
call for papers for the Digital Cultures conference[4] in Lüneburg
that led to the texts in this book. Future states of trivial machines,
whose behavior, by definition, does not change over time, might

3   The term autopoiesis (from Greek αὐτο- [auto-], meaning "self," and ποίησις
    [poiesis], meaning "creation, production") refers to a system capable of
    reproducing and maintaining itself. The term was introduced in 1972 by
    Chilean biologists Humberto Maturana and Francisco Varela to define the
    self-maintaining processes of living organisms. The concept has been also
    applied to psychic and social systems. For more details see, e.g., Köck (1993).

4   Digital Cultures: Knowledge / Culture / Technology, Leuphana University
    Lüneburg, September 19–22, 2018.

 be predictable, but socio-technical-cultural systems are non-trivial machines. Nontrivial machines do have a history that cannot be neglected, and we certainly should not entertain the idea of an "end of history" as suggested by Fukuyama (1992). The behavior of nontrivial machines depends on their history and is irreversible in time. They remain black boxes. Even more disturbing: their development is evolutionary—seemingly "causal" explanations can at best be delivered afterwards. Attempts at generalizing these post-hoc explanations frequently lead to Rolf Nohr's assertion with respect to business simulation projects in "Preferable Futures" on page 75 of this book: "The (uncertain) future imploded into a kind of 'feedback-effected present' in which tendencies were intensified or subdued. Future was hedged and immobilized." Or, in a pointed interpretation with regard to the subject at hand: data-driven AI exposes the prejudices and wishful thinking of those who feed it, thus stabilizing social structures and expectations.

We have become increasingly exposed to such AI bias, even in the simple case of Amazon's recommendation engine: past developments are extrapolated into the future. The banal stupidity of the system sometimes feels insulting to independent thinkers. Not even the most comprehensive data resources and the most "intelligent" algorithms would ever be able to produce a *Laplacean Demon*: the map is not the territory. The success of Big Data and AI is necessarily based on faith in continuous trajectories. So, they do not predict futures in a "scientific" way, but they suggest, direct, manipulate, and design futures based on this soporific belief in continuity, thus stabilizing trajectories and path-dependencies. In a sense the algorithms present plausible, even probable (based on the data) and desirable (with respect to the companies' interests) design options. In effect, we can interpret it as an unhealthy, toxic mix of science and political-economic strategy. For an opposing positive and affirmative view of the same phenomenon see, for example, Schmalz and Bram (2019).

Any evolutionary or even revolutionary[5] aspects of socio-cultural-
technical development have to be carefully hidden and denied
in this game. I suppose—aware of the danger of succumbing to
a conspiracy theory—that this is done so as not to question the
prevailing political-economic project of globalization. Outcomes
of these manipulations (called "analyses") are presented as
"scientific," that is, without reasonable alternative.

In fact, with this barely noticeable shift from analytical-
descriptive prediction to normative projection, we have reached
design, albeit in a rather problematic understanding of the term.
As soon as we accept that history, human and social development, proceeds not along stable trajectories but rather in an
evolutionary way, then we have to think more thoroughly about
the conception, potential and limits of design. Two issues are
essential: First, the problem of control (the difficulty of dealing
with irreducible complexity)—system/context distinctions,
boundary judgements determine what we can control and what
we cannot. Second, the problem of prediction (the impossibility
of predicting future states of nontrivial systems)—futures are
an issue of power relations, hegemonic struggles, and decisions
based on value orientations. "Everything that is said is said by an
observer" (Förster 1981)—and some observers are more powerful
than others.

Contextualizing Transformation Design

"The best way to predict the future is to create it" is a statement
frequently attributed to Abraham Lincoln. [6] Design scientist Buck-
minster Fuller and many others have repeated the slogan. So,
if we do not want to accept the predetermined trajectories, we
depend on *the design way* (Nelson and Stolterman 2003), which

---

5   Evolution and revolution are not that different in this context—evolution can
    be very disruptive.
6   References are contradictory, but Lincoln is historically the first to be
    mentioned.

 means to create options, futures in stock, in order not to be taken by surprise too much. And "we" choose what "we" prefer. The central questions seem to be: How do we want to live? How do we create this change?[7]

The following discussion is about contextualizing and thus, in a way, de-mystifying the mega project—at least it appears as such—of transformation design. In my view, this endeavor should not be about introducing or defining a new sub-discipline, such as product, automotive, or fashion design. That would imply an ambitious intention to create a new radical design movement, one associated with highly moral claims of knowing better how to guide humankind on its long and risky way towards a more sustainable future.[8] Looking back, we realize that most of these radical movements have failed or have been replaced by the next big design hype. So, transformation design is not a new discipline, it instead describes an attitude of being fully aware of the factual and ethical implications of living and designing in an accelerated, dramatically fast era of risky change. In other words: We should avoid reification; it is an epistemological (communicative, cultural) project, not an ontological one. The concept should remind us to permanently reconsider what it means to actively intervene in our evolving social, cultural, and natural environments. So, to be very clear: transformation design is a placement, not a category (Jonas et al. 2016, 13–15).

Design scientist, AI pioneer, and famous economist Herbert Simon first presented his *Sciences of the Artificial* in 1969. The book, one of the few fundamental and substantial contributions in design, addresses two important aspects that complement the aforementioned issues, namely the problem of control and

7   So far, I have not elaborated on the big challenges (climate change, global injustice, etc.) we are facing. All this, including the allegedly compelling remedies for it (growth, competition, technological progress, more of the same) is the implicit background against which I argue.

8   The *Transition Design* project at Carnegie Mellon University appears to be of this kind: http://transitiondesign.net.

the problem of prediction, in a more design-specific way. The first aspect he addresses is the interface concept, meaning that design creates the interfaces between artefacts (the "inner systems") and the contexts (the "outer systems") in which they have to function and survive (Simon [1969] 1996, 6). We need methodologies that help us deal with systemic complexity and issues of boundary judgment[9] in order to properly define and represent the scope of our design task. The second aspect is the broad definition of design that means to devise courses of action that aim to transfer existing situations into preferred ones (111). We conceive futures based on value judgments about these futures. In epistemological terms this implies that we no longer act as distant, "objective" observers but as situated participants who hold a specific stake in the situation. We are being designed at the same time as we are designing, and have to carefully reflect on our respective roles and positions in the inquiring system. Our stance must be made explicit.

Scope and Stance in Transformation Design

With reference to Alain Findeli (Findeli and Bousbaki 2005, Findeli 2010), we have to consider the scope of our subject matter, which is a complex, hybrid mix of material and immaterial entities and actors. And we have to consider the stance of the designing / inquiring system, which once might have been the individual author designer or the disembodied Cartesian observer,[10] but is now a hybrid mix of individual and collective

9   Boundary judgement or boundary critique (BC) is the concept in critical systems heuristics that, according to Werner Ulrich, states that "both the meaning and the validity of professional propositions always depend on boundary judgments as to what 'facts' (observation) and 'norms' (valuation standards) are to be considered relevant" or not. See https://wulrich.com/boundary_critique.html, accessed March 26, 2020.

10   In Western scientific ontology, all human perceptions are referred to a viewpoint of Cartesian positional identity. This observer has been traditionally treated as real, the viewer of external objective reality. In many other philosophical, religious, mystical, or spiritual systems of knowing based on

knowledges, motivations, intentions, interests, and power constellations. Statements of objective truths are, at best, replaced by negotiations in a situation of "epistemic democracy" (Dewey 1916), which defends the capacity of the educated and informed "many" to make correct decisions and seeks to justify democracy by reference to this ability. More realistically, or, typically, truth claims are replaced by conflict and fierce struggle. Both the definitions of power regarding scope and the freedom of decision-making regarding stance are issues of power relationships. Power relations determine what can be considered changeable in a problem situation. And power relations determine which goals are acceptable and enforceable. Against this background we have to reflect and decide whether, in transformative processes, we consider the widest possible boundaries as negotiable or as fixed. Taking them as negotiable implies questioning the dominant regime of market society with its paradigm of continuous growth by means of production and consumption, no matter what is produced and consumed, and the paradigm of the one-world model of global development—the Global North determines the rules; the Global South has to adopt them (Escobar 2018).

Questioning these paradigms may appear to be designers' hubris. On the other hand, if we take these conditions for granted, we will be mentally and discursively caught in the trivial, technocratic commonplace rhetoric of "change," which tells us to adapt our values and our ways of living and working to the supposedly unavoidable "challenges" of global economic competition and the imperatives of growth. In fact, the sole aim of such "change" is to stabilize business as usual as long as possible and prevent any fundamental change in our ideas of global futures. Just when we assume that design does not actively change the world—even if some conceive of themselves as design activists—but creates and offers options and images and narratives that present

introspective techniques of producing "oceanic" experience, it is regarded as virtual and the objective/subjective antithesis as contingent.

possible and desirable changes, then we should try hard to avoid self-imposed thinking restrictions of any kind. Herbert Simon characterized social design as a kind of "mental window-shopping" ([1969] 1996, 164): "[P]urchases do not have to be made to draw benefit from it." In other words, visions are unlimited. It is our task to make proposals and put them forward for discussion. It is not actually our task to realize them. So what?

Hubris and Modesty: A Delicate Tightrope Walk

Coming back to the initial question regarding design's potential to exert political influence. I argued that we are not considering transformation design as a new well-defined discipline, but that we are instead re-considering design activities under the challenging conditions of the Great Transformation (Polanyi 1944). Some may know my hypothesis (Jonas 2010) that there is no progress in design, meaning that design, as the interface-building discipline operating in the co-evolutionary space between systems and their contexts, has to struggle hard in order to keep abreast of the dramatic changes around us. On that note I think it is time to turn things upside down and argue that transformation design is the most general, the overall, the fundamental concept, even if it is not much more than a vague and incompletely defined attitude. All more specific "tastes" of design (dealing with products, cars, fashion, interfaces, etc.) are sub-fields, limited in scope and stance, which can be derived from the basic concept: transformation design is the new normal design.

But how is this compatible with Horst Rittel's call for "a certain modesty in design" (Reuter and Jonas 2013) and with Heinz von Förster's reminder to keep ethics implicit (Förster 1993, 1995)?[11]

11   Von Förster formulated the following rule: "For any discourse, I may have—say, in science, philosophy, epistemology, therapy, etc.—to master the use of my language so that ethics is implicit. What do I mean by that? I mean by that

If we claim that transformation design is the new normal, could it be that we are even more susceptible to hubris and mystify design's potential even more? A strange paradox seems to arise here. Maybe modest hubris has to be cultivated in order to transform established mindsets. Transformation design is the new normal, but at the same time we have to question its goal-oriented problem-solving potential and its competence to answer the big questions it raises.[12]

If we consider transformative design not only as an attitude, but rather as a theory and methodology to devise change for the better in society, then we have to thoroughly reflect on and debate design's agencies at the intersection of bottom-up processes, public institutions, and formalized politics. An essential point seems to be the unclear distinction between politics and the political (Herlo et al. 2017). In German political theory, politics has been conceptualized as a highly formalized functional system that includes state, government, and parties, dealing with the question of how to organize decision processes, and how this organization can be justified. The broader concept of the political points to more philosophical questions about the nature of the political and the political dimension of the social (Machart 2010).[13] It is undisputed that design has political implications in this latter respect.

to let language and action ride on an underground river of ethics, and to see to it that one is not thrown off, so that ethics does not become explicit, and so that language does not degenerate into moralization." See https://stream.syscoi.com/2018/10/21/ethics-and-second-order-cybernetics-heinz-von-foerster/, accessed January 14, 2023.

12   A bit like romantic irony, which is an attitude of detached skepticism adopted by an author towards his or her own work, typically manifesting in literary self-consciousness and critical self-reflection.

13   Two tradition lines can be distinguished in the concept of the political: the associative and the dissociative line, which can be related to Hannah Arendt and Carl Schmitt. Arendt formulates an associative theory of the political, which defines the political as a free, communicative space of co-operation, whereas Schmitt, on the other hand, emphasizes the dissociative aspect which conceives the political as an area of power and conflict (based on the

In any case, the debate raises questions such as: How radical should design be? How political can/should design education be, and how political is it permitted to be? And how does it work in practice? Again: only unanswerable questions are legitimate! It seems we are performing an exciting tightrope walk between modesty and hubris, especially when dealing with the political.

Deficits and Blind Spots in Dealing with "the Political"

Beside the missing reflection on political theory there are specific designerly weaknesses. Projects like those presented in the *"Uncertain Futures"* book (Förster et al. 2018), reveal theoretical and practical deficits. Although we love to talk about multiple futures and potentialities, the debate is often narrow-minded and highly moral, obviously suffering from the self-imposed burden of world rescue, which seems to be a kind of tacit consensus in the community. As though we knew better than others what should be achieved by means of our interventions. And as though it was our own responsibility to implement these options. To be very clear at this point: design is necessarily normative because it is about ways of transforming existing situations. However, this normativity, which is reflected on and negotiated in the process, must be clearly distinguished from a presupposed, narrow, and often barely reflected on morality based on fixed codes.

The MA in Transformation Design at Braunschweig University of Art explicitly claims "to reflect on, initiate, design change processes," which clearly touches on the political. First, reflection: this is unproblematic because it is harmless (as long as it does not dangerously radicalize thinking). Second, to (co-) design: according to Simon ([1969] 1996) "[t]o design is to devise courses

notion of antagonism). Chantal Mouffe (2005), on the other hand, developed the concept of agonism, in which opponents recognize the legitimacy of the "other," envisioning the implementation of the opponents' projects.

of action aimed at changing existing situations into preferred ones." To devise courses of action does not necessarily mean to implement them. So, also rather unproblematic, if taken seriously. Design activists still reject this restriction. Third, to initiate: this is perhaps the most delicate term, where one comes closest to the—in my view —misunderstanding of designers doing practical politics. Real-world laboratories (*Reallabore* in German) can possibly be seen as—always revisable—first steps towards the initiation of practical political activities.

In practical terms designers tend to overestimate the effects of their own contributions. Reports on social design projects (Förster et al. 2018) often show a naïve worldview in tackling the problems and a frightening triviality in the results; fashionable catchwords like sharing, collaboration, participation, empowerment, etc. are too inflationary. Subsequent robust evaluations of the alleged improvements are mostly missing. In their sometimes blind search for harmony and world salvation, designers frequently neglect or ignore the complex nature of the human psyche and of social communities with all their stupidity and selfishness. They seem to work from the assumption that humans are basically good. Which they are obviously not! Human beings are good and bad and mostly mean (in both meanings of the term). And societies are complex and full of paradox and conflict. And it is these hegemonic struggles and power conflicts that seem to be essential for a productive democratic culture (Mouffe 2005).

My critique can be summarized as follows: what is missing is an advanced and appropriate systemic social theory of design that complements the delicate normative stance. I propose, therefore, to relate transformative design to sociological systems theory (Luhmann 1995), with a special focus on three topics: systems in an autopoietic understanding, communication as a process of triple selection, and evolution as the contextual condition. Which means that relevant social and psychic systems cannot control but rather irritate each other, that communication is a highly risky

sequential process of information, utterance, and understanding,
and that cultural evolution has to be considered as evolutionary,
with purposive planning always remaining the rare exception.
In this way, the problems of control and prediction mentioned
above would at least theoretically be framed and thus connect-
able for further theoretical considerations.[14]

Who is the Client? And where is the Designer?

The considerations above on the potentials and limits of design
approaches in broader social and political contexts are closely
related to Simon's question, "Who is the client?" in Chapter 6
"Social Planning: Designing the Evolving Artifact" in *Sciences of the
Artificial*. The essential question is whether there is still anything
like the classic design client here. Simon argues regarding
"society as the client" ([1969] 1996, 153): "It may seem obvious
that all ambiguities should be resolved by identifying the client
with the whole society. That would be a clear-cut solution in a
world without conflict of interest or uncertainty in professional
judgement." But "[t]he members of an organization or a society
for whom plans are made are not passive instruments, but are
themselves designers who are seeking to use the system to further their own goals."

One may object that in our "progressive" understanding of
design, plans are not made for but with people. This is what
Valerie Brown (2010) addresses and elaborates in her reflections
on the power relationships between the researcher and the community, or the designer and those affected by the design. She
distinguishes six qualities:

- to work on a community: as observer, external planner
- to work for a community: as employee

14   For more details regarding this critique of naïve designerly worldviews see
       Jonas (2019, 2020).

- to work on behalf of a community: as delegate
- to work with a community: in partnership
- to work within a community: sharing their values and aims
- to work as a community: belonging to the community

This sequence opens up a continuum between the one extreme of the expert designer or Cartesian inquirer who works on a community from the position of an external observer, and the other extreme of the inquiring community, which means to work as a community, being part of the design situation. The latter comes close to John Dewey's ideal of "epistemic democracy" (Dewey 1916) as a collective exercise in practical intelligence, which describes the idea that inquiry and decision making in general, including scientific inquiry, not just political inquiry and decision making, are or should be democratic in character. In the first case (to work on a community) we have design as consultant, contractor, or advisor of politics, developing options, narratives, moderating, facilitating decision-making processes for others, but not deciding. Value conflicts are likely to occur with the professional expert, which is well-known in the profession: does what I'm doing still align with my conscience? In the second case (working as a community), the individual design researcher acts as a politically and socially responsible individual. Role conflicts between professional and citizen are likely to occur, which is new and has to be reflected on. New role models show up: the citizen designer or the designing citizen that re-enact 1970s utopian ideas about the vanishing of expert cultures, even social functional systems, in the digital age.[15]

(Transformation) Design is Political but it does not do Politics

My hypothesis for the moment is: design is political but it does not do politics! Design's main tasks are to develop options, to

15   See for example John Christopher Jones' "creative democracy" (2000).

increase the variety of choices, to cultivate its role as scout, jester,
and agent provocateur for the public (Dunne & Raby 2013).

Simon argues ([1969] 1996, 163):

> One desideratum would be a world offering as many
> alternatives as possible to future decision makers, avoiding
> irreversible commitments that they cannot undo. [...] The act
> of envisioning possibilities and elaborating them is itself a
> pleasurable and valuable experience. Just as realized plans
> may be a source of new experience, so new prospects are
> opened up at each step in the process of design. Designing
> is a kind of mental window shopping. [...] One can envisage
> a future, however, in which our main interest in both science
> and design will lie in what they teach us about the world
> and not in what they allow us to do to the world. Design like
> science is a tool for understanding as well as for acting.

In my own words: it is necessary to rethink the balance between
reflection and action in design. In this respect I fully agree with
Carl Di Salvo (2012):

> Simply stated, the purpose of political design is to do the
> work of agonism. This means first and foremost it does the
> work of creating spaces for revealing and confronting power
> relations, i.e., it creates spaces of contest. This occurs both in
> and through the objects and processes of design: the objects
> and processes of design are both the site and means of
> agonistic pluralism.

Sociologist Dirk Baecker (2000) called design the expert discipline for dealing with not-knowing. His more recent, slightly
paradoxical dictum of design as a means of "Uncertainty Absorption in the Next Society" (Baecker 2015) points in a promising
direction. He argues that today we know about the contingency
of all options that we are facing. Design does not obscure this
uncertainty but makes it explicit and reflective. That (ironic) trans-
parency is precisely why it contributes to uncertainty absorption.

Conclusion 1: Designing as "Muddling Through"

Muddling through is, in the context of organizational theory, not a pejorative or even negative concept. It was first used as a theoretical term in management science (Charles E. Lindblom 1959, 1979). The starting point of Lindblom's reflections was the finiteness of any holistic view of a social system. Overall strategic plans therefore necessarily lead to unexpected and undesirable (secondary) consequences in the case of direct implementation. He argues for incrementalism, gradualism, muddling through as a process of negotiation.[16] My two programmatic hypotheses address this issue:

1. Re-conceptualize and broaden the understanding of design. From shaping artefacts to creating dialogical/agonistic processes of exploring and conceiving preferable futures. Call this activity transformative design or policy advice or muddling through or whatever. What actually happens is usually muddling through anyway.
2. Turn from technocratic prediction (planning/problem-solving) to designerly projection (futures studies has taken this turn already). That is, establish an experimental, iterative culture of curiosity. Introduce playfulness and create smaller-scale playgrounds and arenas of trial and error. Be radical on the playground—incremental in the real world.

16 Lindblom developed the theory of incrementalism in policy and decision-making, which takes a "baby-steps," "Muddling Through" or "Echternach Theory" approach to decision-making processes. In it, policy change is mostly evolutionary rather than revolutionary. He came to this view through his studies of welfare policies and trade unions throughout the industrialized world. These views are set out in two articles, separated by twenty years: "The Science Of 'Muddling Through'" (1959) and "Still Muddling, Not yet through" (1979), both published in *Public Administration Review*. A good overview can be found at https://en.wikipedia.org/wiki/Charles_E._Lindblom, accessed December 3, 2021.

Isabelle Stengers (2015, 9) talks about "the divorce between capitalism and the great tale of progress." And she notes the emergence of "knowledge economies," those questionable but powerful hybrids of science and economy, mentioned at the beginning. So, the normative core of this project, while remaining aware of the danger of falling victim to the blind spot of ideological hubris, is the task of re-embedding the markets, i.e., to transform our present market society into a society with markets (Polanyi 1944). We should consider that as the possibly unattainable but still necessary vision.

Conclusion 2: Serenity and Playfulness Instead of Strained Hubris

Herbert Simon's ([1969] 1996: 163, 164) description is more relaxed:

> The idea of final goals is inconsistent with our limited ability to foretell or determine the future. The result of our actions is to establish initial conditions for the next succeeding stage of action. What we call 'final' goals are in fact criteria for choosing the initial conditions that we will leave to our successors.

According to Bruno Latour, design may be conceived as the appropriate substitute for the ambitious and now obsolete modernist mega-projects of technological progress, social revolution, and ultimate modernization. We should take his question seriously (2013, 23), "In other words, why not transform this whole business of recalling modernity into a grand question of design?" Or, to avoid the overused and still somehow suspiciously cocky term "design," let's call it Happily Muddling Through. The supposed contradiction in the simultaneous endorsement of Luhmann (see above) and Latour can be countered as follows: Latour's suggested imperative (recalling modernity by design), considered within Luhmann's descriptive system-theoretical framework conditions (the autopoietic character of social systems, the improbability of successful communication, and the evolutionary nature of social developments) leads to the pragmatic consequence of promoting Muddling Through as a strategic guideline. Admittedly a very pragmatic, designerly—and again slightly ironic—way of thinking, deliberately and happily disrespecting the boundaries between supposedly sharply separated theoretical areas.

So, instead of regarding design as strained social activism I suggest conceiving it as a discipline, or an un-discipline, of playing with un/certainty: certain certainties, uncertain certainties, certain uncertainties, uncertain uncertainties, critical uncertainties. . . .

Let's play with supposedly fixed realities, with supposedly fixed epistemic standards that we sometimes take too uncritically from the sciences, with our own roles in design situations. For example, cultivate the role as jester (Jones 2000). Overcome the strained fixation on desired utopias or dystopias to be avoided in favor of the playful design of mind-opening heterotopias, which can be discussed publicly (Foucault 1990). This may relieve design (at least a bit) of the moral burden of rescuing the world.

And, finally, it allows us to do some good for ourselves. Otl Aicher notes: "in designing, people come into their own. otherwise they remain civil servants." In German (Aicher 1991: 195): „im entwerfen kommt der mensch zu sich selbst. anders bleibt er beamter."

References

Aicher, Otl. 1991. "die welt als entwurf". In *die welt als entwurf*, 185–96. Berlin: Ernst & Sohn. A PDF of the english translation by Michael Robinson can be found here: http://s3.amazonaws.com/arena-attachments/2733682/10dcdf4245d3d28ef2e8a 8ba007e37be.pdf?1537377068.
Baecker, Dirk. 2000. "Wie steht es mit dem Willen Allahs?" *Zeitschrift für Rechtssoziologie* (21) 1: 145-76.

Baecker, Dirk.2015. "Design Trust: Uncertainty Absorption in the Next Society".
    Merkur (69) 799: 89–97.
Brown, Valerie A. 2010. "Collective Inquiry and Its Wicked Problems". In *Tackling
    Wicked Problems through the Transdisciplinary Imagination*, edited by Valerie A.
    Brown, John A. Harris, and Jacqueline Y. Russell, 61–83. London: Earthscan.
Dewey, John. 1916. *Democracy and Education*. New York: The Macmillan Company.
Di Salvo, Carl. 2012. *Adversarial Design*. Cambridge, MA: MIT Press
Dunne, Anthony, and Fiona Raby. 2013. *Speculative Everything: Design, Fiction, and
    Social Dreaming*. Cambridge, MA: MIT Press.
Escobar, Arturo. 2018. *Farewell to Development*. Accessed October 16, 2018. http://
    greattransition.org/publication/farewell-to-development.
Findeli, Alain, and Rabah Bousbaki. 2005. "L'éclipse de l'objet dans les theories du
    projet en design". *The Design Journal* (8) 3: 35–49.
Findeli, Alain. 2010. "Searching for Design Research Questions: Some Conceptual
    clarifications". In *Questions, Hypotheses & Conjectures*, edited by Rosan Chow,
    Wolfgang Jonas, and Gesche Joost, #–#. #: Xlibris Corp.
Förster, Heinz von. 1981. *Observing Systems*. Seaside, CA: Intersystems Publications
Förster, Heinz von. 1993. *KybernEthik*. Berlin: Merve.
Förster, Heinz von. 1995. "Ethics and Second-Order Cybernetics". *Stanford
    Humanities Review* (4) 2: 308–19.
Förster, Marius, Saskia Hebert, Mona Hofmann, and Wolfgang Jonas, eds. 2018. *Un/
    Certain Futures: Rollen des Designs in gesellschaftlichen Transformationsprozessen*.
    Bielefeld: transcript.
Foucault, Michel. 1990. "Andere Räume." In: *Aisthesis: Wahrnehmung heute oder Per-
    spektiven einer anderen Ästhetik*, edited by Karlheinz Barck u.a., 34–46. Leipzig:
    Reclam.
Fukuyama, Francis. 1992. *The End of History and the Last Man*. New York: Free Press.
Herlo, Bianca, Andreas Unteidig, Wolfgang Jonas, and Idil Gaziulusoy. 2017. "Per-
    spectives on Socially and Politically Oriented Practices in Design: A Discussion-
    based Workshop." *Proceedings of EAD2017*. Rome.
Jonas, Wolfgang. 2010. „Designwissenschaft als Netz von Theorien und Akteuren—10
    Anmerkungen." In *Positionen zur Designwissenschaft*, edited by Felicidad Romero-
    Tejedor and Wolfgang Jonas, 79–85. Kassel: Kassel University Press.
Jonas, Wolfgang. 2019. "Design Cybernetics: Concluding Remarks from a Semi-
    External Perspective". In *Design Cybernetics: Navigating the New*, edited by
    Thomas Fischer and Christiane M. Herr, 281–98. Cham: Springer.
Jonas, Wolfgang. 2020. "On Futures, Un/Certainties, Design Hubris and Moralityor: A
    Cautious Plea for Reflection and Moral Disarmament in Transformation Design".
    Journal of Design Thinking (1) 1: 81–87. Accessed February 21, 2022, https://jdt.
    ut.ac.ir/article_76039_abf26fe24a47e2c5071b1f47d9f40ce1.pdf.
Jonas, Wolfgang, Sarah Zerwas, and Kristof von Anshelm, eds. 2016. *Transformation
    Design: Perspectives on a New Design Attitude*. Basel: Birkhäuser.
Jones, John Christopher. 2000. *The Internet and Everyone*. London: Ellipsis.
Köck, Wolfgang K. 1993. „Autopoiese, Kognition und Kommunikation: Einige
    kritische Bemerkungen zu Humberto R. Maturanas Bio-Epistemologie und

ihren Konsequenzen." In *Zur Biologie der Kognition: Ein Gespräch mit Humberto R. Maturana und Beiträge zur Diskussion seines Werkes*, edited by Volker Riegas and Christian Vetter, 159–88. Frankfurt am Main: Suhrkamp.

Latour, Bruno. 2013. *An Inquiry into Modes of Existence: An Anthropology of the Moderns*. Cambridge, MA: Harvard University Press

Lindblom, Charles E. 1959. "The Science of 'Muddling Through'". *Public Administration Review* (19) 2: 79–88.

Lindblom, Charles E. 1979. "Still Muddling, Not yet through". *Public Administration Review* (39) 6: 517–26.

Luhmann, Niklas. 1995. *Social Systems*. Stanford: Stanford University Press.

Machart, Oliver. 2010. *Die politische Differenz*. Berlin: Suhrkamp.

Mouffe, Chantal. 2005. *On the Political*. London: Routledge.

Nelson, Harold G., and Erik Stolterman. 2003. *The Design Way: Intentional Change in an Unpredictable World*. Englewood Cliffs, NJ: Educational Technology Publications.

Polanyi, Karl Paul. 1944. *The Great Transformation: The Political and Economic Origins of Our Time*. Boston: Beacon Press.

Reuter, Wolf D., and Wolfgang Jonas, eds. 2013. *Horst Rittel: Thinking Design. Transdisziplinäre Konzepte für Planer und Entwerfer*. Basel: Birkhäuser.

Schmalz, Martin, and Uri Bram. 2019. *The Business of Big Data: How to Create Lasting Value in the Age of AI*. Accessed November 30, 2021, http://www.thebusinessofbigdata.com.

Simon, Herbert A. (1969) 1996. *The Sciences of the Artificial*. Cambridge, MA: MIT Press.

Stengers, Isabelle. 2015. *In Catastrophic Times: Resisting the Coming Barbarism*. London: Open Humanities Press / Lüneburg: meson press.

BUSINESS SIMULATIONS

MODEL THEORY

CLUB OF ROME

SIMULATION

PREDICTABILITY

3

The Rise of Business Simulations and the Elimination of Uncertainty

Rolf F. Nohr

A "future prediction" is, more or less, only a narrowing of the future driven by a continuation of the present in the forecast. Big data and predictive analytics promise prediction and the elimination of contingency. But forecasting often means to extend the current present into the future. This chapter will demonstrate—with the example of business simulations from the 1950s to 1970s—how an ensemble of technologies and discursive practices tried to predict and immobilize the future. But the outcomes of these projects were contrary: the (uncertain) future imploded into a kind of "feedback-effected present" in which tendencies were intensified or subdued. The future was hedged and immobilized.

At best we live in a world of uncertain future.
The aim of science has always been towards
lessening this uncertainty.
— Morris Asimow (1959)[1]

The Asimow quote above is from one of the earliest academic discussions on management games. The business simulations and management simulation games discussed at that time will be used in this essay as specific examples to trace the origins of a specific discursive rationality in the 1950s to 1970s. This is based on the thesis that business simulations (Bsims), which companies installed on early main frame computers (such as the IBM 650) and used as training and development tools, resulted in a specific understanding of (computer-based) prognostics and planning, which, once revealed, shaped the following decades. In addition to its use as a specific training tool, when combined with other epistemological tools and epistemologies, that constellation of knowledge became "fixed," resulting in a perspective that focused on minimizing contingency, which established the idea that the future was manageable.[2] However, this essay aims to use the example of Bsims to take a closer look at the general, historical development of a specific rationality in terms of managing the future. By looking at Bsims' specific access to the future, I aim to outline how, at a defined point the early postwar period, specific (prognostic) actions and specific media technology (first and foremost: computers) developed a certain praxeology and operational rationality with regard to managing contingency, which are still effective today. The relatively marginal example of Bsims allows us to easily draw a connecting line to the fantasies

1   Cited in Fessler, Saunders, and Steele (1959, V-3).
2   This text is an abstract of the Nohr 2019 publication. Each of the theses and reconstructions in the following discussion is described there in more detail, soundly supported by the respective historical source material.

of total enterprise simulations and the prognostic components of the Club of Rome's *The Limits to Growth* report. However, these probes, intended as examples, prove significant once we look at the overall context (including that of this book) and ask how we tame, limit, or predict the future today.

So what are Bsims, exactly? The transition from wartime economy to civil business after the end of World War II resulted in great shifts in the field of business management, caused by the changing cultural framework conditions as well as upheavals in economic order (the key term here is the beginning of globalized markets). One significant example of this is the "birth" of the manager, meaning the renunciation of traditional, "patriarchal" corporate management and the trend towards the concept of allowing companies to be managed by professionally trained executives. Training for these professional managers and "helmsmen" in particular prompted the founding of business schools[3] at universities—and this upheaval is significantly inter-woven with the development of business science (as a concept of the ability to rationally manage and research economic activity).

In this light, companies established staff development instruments. Training and development systems, recruiting, and assessments are all methods that originated in this period. The most advanced educational tools were simulation games and models, by means of which middle and upper management were to train and improve their decision-making skills.

The *Top Management Decision Simulation* is generally considered the first Bsims geared exclusively towards non-military users (or rather, the first exclusively market-oriented Bsims). This simu-lation was developed by the American Management Association

---

3   It is important to note that the earliest business schools, including Harvard Business School, were founded in the early twentieth century. However, it is also evident that, particularly in the USA, business simulations were quickly and broadly adopted as a training tool in business schools (see for example Busse von Colbe/Perlitz 1978, 145)

Fig. 1: Gaming situation within the *Top Management Decision Simulation* (around 1956) (source: Ricciardi et al. 1957, 12)

(AMA) in cooperation with a consultancy, Booz Allen Hamilton, and a think tank, RAND Corporation. The training game was developed in 1956, introduced to the public in May 1957, and used as part of an AMA training course at Saranac Lake (New York) from September 1957 on (see Ricciardi et al. 1957 and fig. 1). The *Top Management Decision Simulation* is mostly seen as a direct successor of military simulation games and is therefore also described as a "kind of war school for business executives" (Cohen and Rheman 1961, 134–35). Initially, the AMA game was designed to be calculated by desk calculators. However, it was installed on an IBM 650 during the development process, which

reduced computing time per game period from 45 minutes to five
(Schmidt 1963, 25). In parallel, a second "first" Bsims was created, which in a sense can be seen as an "anti-theses": the *Business Management Game*, a purely manual game that picked up on previous traditions. An interesting question (and one which this paper will not be able to conclusively answer) is how this manual game relates to the AMA game. It is a straightforward board game with a strong focus on aspects of the turnover of capital goods. The *Harvard Business Review* offered the game (including instructions, a reprint of Andlinger's associated publication in the *Harvard Business Review*, decision-making sheets, and game plans) for one dollar (Andlinger 1958, 125). However, both games represent prototypes for other simulations: the AMA game in terms of computer-based simulations, the Andlinger game in terms of (cheaper) "role-playing games."

Subsequently, business simulations became significant development tools in companies and universities and, starting in the USA, rapidly spread throughout the world.[4] Accordingly, the Federal Republic of Germany experienced a Bsims boom in the early 1960s, initially due to transnational companies (such as IBM) implementing and translating American models, followed by genuine German models shortly after. Tailored to the Federal Republic of Germany's specific economic area, these games swiftly achieved similar importance when training young corporate talent. These Bsims were closely connected to the independent, company-related development sector that arose in the FRG from the 1960s on (for example the *Baden-Badener Unternehmensgespräche*, the *Wuppertaler Kreis* or the *Universitätsseminar der Wirtschaft* in Cologne).

---

4   Slightly detached from this, a history of business simulations could be written about economic simulation games in the Soviet Union as well as other countries of the Eastern Bloc. Though it might seem we would find—supposedly—different types of economic rationality and management fantasies, such as a planned economy (for example, Assa 1982), we can, however, observe a high commensurability in models and approaches discussed in the socialist area with discourses in North America and the FRG.

At their core, Bsims are collections of specific algorithms that allow us to describe certain market mechanisms. A typical scenario is an oligopolistic market situation, or in other words, a market with few competitors, into which we introduce consumer goods using various strategies and production decisions. The aim of the competing players is to expand market power, optimize profit figures, reduce production costs, qualify staff, etc.

Generally, Bsims are turn-based games. After an introductory briefing, game participants are presented with a narrative setting within which they are given a set of parameters. The players assume defined roles or represent specific responsibilities within their fictional company. Individually or in groups, they must make decisions for the next round of the game, which in the majority of cases are coded numerically: determining investment volumes, the number of employees, the quantity of production material that is to be purchased and the production rate. Once these numbers have been determined, they are entered into the algorithm at the end of the decision-making round. In most simulation games, this algorithm is executed via a computer. The resulting output is fed back to the players and is the basis for the next round. After a previously defined number of iterations, a final calculation is made. The umpires then provide a debriefing based on the ultimate player performance.

Initially, the scenarios outlined by these games are more or less fictional situations. However, the intent is that these can be applied to existing companies, markets, and macro-economies at any time. On the one hand, the idea of a Bsims is to place players in a more or less fictional situation. However, on the other, the players orient their actions on their (more or less professional) everyday knowledge and thus go beyond the fiction. The desired learning and training effect results from the comparison of one's own actions within a fictional scenario with potential knowledge gained in a "real, non-ludic world." The nature of the exercise provokes the "ludic" aspect: the model's reductive situation aims to achieve a certain distance from reality while at the same time enforcing reality by this exact reduction, thus staging it as manageable. Besides the "as-if" component, the conditions for winning, which are openly defined at all times, are what allow the Bsims to be (competitive) games: winning is everything.

At first glance, we could therefore assume that in the end, Bsims are scenarios in which managers can prepare for the challenges of a globalized world, in a playful manner and aided by computers. However, what may initially look like an economic training simulator proves to be far more than that on closer inspection. In simulation games such as these, the players' dimensions of action comprise acting in scenarios. To put it simply, management simulations require players to extrapolate possible futures from a modeled present, and from this range of futures select one or several that appear desirable (and that are compatible with the game's conditions for winning). In a second step, players define paths and decisions that transform the model present into the desired model condition and align the actions of the game in way that ensures they approach this condition, step by step and round by round.

In this respect, Bsims are not merely devices to train decision making but a practice sphere in which to rehearse and test prognostics of future developments. This process of playing simulations enabled players to develop and hone an entirely new rationality that they simultaneously rehearsed and adapted—and that has continued through history as a discursive trail. This resulted in a specific rationality, an archaeological trail that far exceeds genuine simulation games and continues to be effective to this day. However, in the following analysis I do not wish to discuss the repercussions of this rationality and put them into context with today's debates on serious games and gamification. Rather, I aim to take a more detailed look at some of the constellations that enabled players to think, train, and develop within the Bsims at that time. Which specific knowledge did Bsims aim to make accessible, to convey?

Model Theory

One of the key paradigms that contributed to the effectiveness and assertion of Bsims is the concept of mathematical modelability. The models were not intended to exclusively run practice scenarios. Instead, they initially genuinely arose from the idea of making companies themselves calculable and describable (see the paragraph on total enterprise simulations below). Models and simulations presented a new descriptive language that allowed economic theory and the (young) business sciences to describe economic actions in the context of mathematical predictability and that furthermore enabled economic theories to be formulated as part of a quantifying and empirical endeavor in the first place. Mathematical models are the core of any business simulation and models are the operative sphere in which the company's development is to be predicted. Models are tools that act as statistic, stochastic, simulative or algorithmic practice and as such aim to help make the contingency of the future manageable.

The model theory boom (see, for example, Stachowiak 1973) that developed from the 1950s onward is reflected in Bsims as well as in a specific way of thinking about the operational functionality of the economic itself. The adjacent figure (fig. 2) shows the analog MONIAC computer: it was a device intended to make the complex interdependencies of a (Keynesian) closed market comprehensible and perceptible with regard to price development (Brainard and Scarf 2000). It refers to a model designed by Irving Fisher (one of the main representatives of neoclassical economics) in his dissertation.[5] This model conceptualizes the market as a complex system of hydraulic forces, modeling the idea (or metaphor) of compensation and balance, an idea of recurring import for economics that is made accessible via the reduction and transformation of water's flow, controls, and pipes, while

5   *Mathematical Investigations in the Theory of Value and Prices* (Yale 1892).

Fig. 2: A.W.H. Phillips with the MONIAC (around 1958–67). (Source: © London School of Economics; taken from: https://en.wikipedia.org/wiki/Hydraulic_macroeconomics, accessed April 9, 2019.)

at the same time providing prognostic information on complex interdependencies (see, for example, Adelman 1972, 214–16).

Examples like this one illustrate that Bsims not only strive to make the present manageable (by implementing a strict set of rules in the gaming situation) but at the same time access the future and try to make the contingency of things to come manageable by means of extrapolation methods. At a mathematical level, probability theory and statistics are the foundation for this (besides model theory). Markov chains are a significant example. A Markov chain is a specific stochastic term that is defined by the fact that knowledge of a limited amount of information allows us to make predictions on the future development of a system that are just as good as those made when we have knowledge of the entire amount of information related to the process (Giesen 1967, 1). When combined with the Monte Carlo principle, for example, in which suitable algorithms calculate seemingly random figures (Grüne-Yanoff and Weirich 2010), this results in mathematical description systems that use statistical normal distributions and average value calculations to attempt to make changes in the conditions of systems calculable. The most prominent example of mathematically generated rational model spheres is certainly the mathematic game theory developed by Oskar Morgenstern and John von Neumann (1944) that essentially tries to model subjective behavior as rational-strategic decision-making, thus making it calculable. That such approaches were initially conceived as purely mathematical heuristics and that the actors involved focused on the reductive character of modeling is beyond question. However, these theoretic foundations of simulation games and business simulations indicate that, despite all reservations, the ability to reach conclusions about futures is a key driver in dealing with economic models and their use in training.

The Decision-Making Process

Operationally, this elimination of uncertainties essentially aims to provide a solid and scientific foundation for planning and steering while enabling us to control one of the manager's central moments of action: the decision. As a result, simulation games and management simulations focus on decisive actions. In hindsight, the training and development instruments in simulation games can be seen as an early figuration of

creating "entrepreneurial selves," as Ulrich Bröckling (2007)
assessed them. The rehearsal of decision-making skills and—in
escalation—the machine and prognostic-supported assistance in
decision-making processes are to be seen as a radical subjective
technique.

Bsims initially generate a reduced sphere of action in which
the playing subject has to make decisions as if working on an
assembly line (under competitive pressure and time constraints).
This creates pressure to act that requires two things from the
decision-making subject: first, that every decision be geared
towards a rational action directive and must not be made intui-
tively, and second, that decisions can only be made based on an
anticipated assessment of future developments, as demanded by
the specific action rationality of simulation games. If investment
volumes are defined within a simulation game, or if decisions on
future product lines are made, then the playing subject conceptualizes a possible future outcome that these decisions will lead
to. As a result, each decision eliminates potential futures and,
furthermore, excludes pasts—an almost paradoxical situation
(Luhmann 2018).

Beyond their functionality as subjective decision-making
techniques (or as technological formations to rehearse certain
action rationalities), the simulations and models on which Bsims
are based are more than just spheres of action within which their
subjects make decisions: they themselves are tools within the
decision-making process. Bsims simulations not only model the
sphere of action, they can consequently become prognostic tools
themselves. Or they can at least be used as assist systems that
are intended to provide an objectifying foundation within the
decision-making process. In this context, there is but a fine line
between Bsims and Decision Support Systems (DSS).

Without delving too deeply into the history of their development,
DSS can ultimately be seen as an advanced development of management information systems such as those discussed primarily

 within the military-economic field in the USA during the 1960s. Projects were developed in this field that went beyond mere information management systems, the intended use of which was to store and process the required data within the decision-making process. Instead, they were dedicated to the fundamental possibilities of supporting and even automating the decision-making process. The DSS concept is found in Herbert Simon and Allen Newell's *General Problem Solver* as well as in the work of Doug Engelbart (one of the pioneers of personal computers). In 1968, Engelbart proposed a "hyper collaborative knowledge environment system called NLS (for oNLine System)" (Engelbart 1968),[6] the core functionality of which he considered "data driven decision making." Although the NLS initially comes across as an online conferencing and knowledge organization system, Engelbart still viewed his system's main purpose to be a system for real time decision-making (see, for example, Engelbart 1962; see also Burstein and Holsapple 2008, chapter 7).

Scenario Techniques

The development of decision-making assistance systems goes hand in hand with the differentiation of necessary technologies to predict future system developments. Under the umbrella term of scenario techniques, the possibly most durable epistemological perspective was developed from the mid to late 1970s, which fed into the development of Bsims and remains effective to this day. While in the 1950s and 1960s, mathematical approaches for calculating future developments differentiated more and more, the players involved were simultaneously aware that the contingency of the future would not be achieved via calculations alone, and certainly not unambiguously. Despite the euphoria created by the possibilities and methods of statistic, stochastic, and prognostic calculation methods, the scientists involved were constantly

6   Engelbart's presentation can be accessed online: http://dougengelbart.org/ content/view/276/000/. Accessed April 9, 2019.

aware that the ideal of determinism and full calculability of the future was just that: an ideal. As a result, they focused their efforts on allowing a plurality of different futures to enter their prognostic methods and to direct their energy more towards methods to evaluate the probability of different futures.

A method emerged for dealing with the objective and empirical weighting of different futures based less on mathematics and more on sociological, political, and behavioral approaches. Especially in connection with the calculable future as negotiated by the models and simulations of Bsims, the idea of scenario research known today (with its funnels and best-and-worst-case scenarios) was not as decisive for the boom in techniques as the concept of operational gaming, which was much closer to the numeric and key indicator-based worlds of Bsims. Operational gaming is a process that is geared much more strongly towards the logic of calculability and aims to find optimum solutions in processes that operate temporally by translating them into game-like situations. Closely related to mathematical game theory, military simulation games, and operations research, the focus of operational gaming lies in the weighting and evaluation of a collection of possible future developments (Cohen and Rhenman 1961, 159). Dry-runs, shake-down cruises, and exploration studies are methods on the basis of which trial and error test runs, exploration, and planning are combined (see Shubik 1974, 8–9, 207).

From the discourse within the Federal Republic of Germany, the work of Horst Koller is among those relevant for this discussion. Very much in the spirit of experimental economics, Koller banks on the option of precise calculability of (market-) economic behavior from an epistemological point of view. In what is known as *"Berechnungsexperimente"* (Koller [1966] 1975, 173–74)—the German version of operational gaming, which translates to "calculatory experiments"—an "experimentalization" of the economy is performed. For Koller, Bsims merely represent a subgroup of the superordinate *"Berechnungsexperimente"* in this context. This means that Bsims (at least those with a more economic-theoretical or scientific-mathematical orientation) belong to the same traditional line from which experimental economics developed. Equally inspired by mathematical game theory, theoreticians such as Heinz Sauermann and Reinhard Selten began to experimentally evaluate economic theories. Experiments were generally used to examine psychologically assessed principles of individual actions in economically relevant decision-making situations (see, for example, Sauermann and Selten 1959). In the course of this, the decision-making processes examined were often abstractly modeled while employing various decision-making and mathematical game theory models and were processed by testers. To this day, experimental economics stand for the "empiricalization" of economics. The specific rationality concept of mathematical game theory contributed to this—and the specific focus simulation games place on the decision-making term and action rationalities that create an (oligopolistic) market as well as the Bsims' model base and experimental setting make it extremely interesting from an experimental economics perspective.

Total Enterprise Simulation

At this point, as we enter the field of experimental epistemologies, the Bsims (and the simulative methods that surround them) leave the pragmatic and functional level. At this "breakage point" of operational gaming in particular, prognostic methods assume a more speculative dimension. In the USA, operational gaming is currently more than just a method used in business economics and macroeconomic studies. It is also the foundation of scenario-based practice games in the political-economic field. An example of this is RAND Corporation, which conducted scenario test runs based on game theory developed by Morgenstern and von Neumann, which aims to predict global political or economic developments including, perhaps most notoriously, studies on thermonuclear warfare options as submitted by

Herman Kahn. Whether we take Kahn's book, *On Thermonuclear War* (1960), as an example or fall back on the idea of total enterprise simulation—which ties in much more neatly with all of the above—we can see the fantasy of total simulatability in each of these projects.

Total enterprise simulations are a consequence of the assumption that full, dynamic, feedback-effected modeling of an enterprise that is as detailed as possible must inevitably have prognostic qualities. If we could depict an enterprise's attributes, relationships, and interdependence precisely enough, this would inevitably allow us to extrapolate the future from this model and thus eliminate the contingency. The aim of such approaches is to create a total model of the enterprise by analyzing and integrating all available data (see, for example, Newell and Meier 1972). Such a "total simulation" obviously depends on (and is limited by) the functionality of the model it is based on. And due to the expected quantitative amount of data, it also depends on its implementability in the computer (Rühl 1961). Therefore, ideas on how to potentially connect Bsims to total enterprise simulation projects always boomed as soon as a breakthrough in hardware or software development was announced (see Witte 1973, 16–18).

In the control fantasies of total simulation, the relation of players and models are reversed: players are no longer participants who confidently make decisions within the symbolic game space (all the while rehearsing how to make decisions) but are now the opposite. Ultimately, the players become merely random elements that, with their non-rational (due to their subjectivity) decisions, contribute a vague and random element to the model, which is precisely what the model requires to uphold its precision. Within the model, the person playing is merely present as a static white noise or random generator.

What is interesting about this fantasy of total predictability and manageability of enterprises (or even macroeconomies) is not so much the fact of its existence but rather the fantasy it emerges from. In fact, there are few examples of functional and operational total enterprise simulations—the most prominent is certainly the Chilean project, *Cybersyn*, from 1977, for which Stafford Beere was responsible. It was possibly also the most questionable project.[7] The 1960s and 1970s saw the establishment of large-scale, macroeconomic models,[8] however, total enterprise simulations that have been employed functionally are rarely mentioned. Still, the idea (or fantasy, or promise) of such total simulatability (even as a mere promotional marketing measure) continues to haunt the entire simulation game scene.[9]

Nevertheless, many sources seem to think that the "utopia" of total simulation was already suspect at the beginning of the investigation period. After all, its claim of depicting every (relevant) aspect of a situation has proven unrealistic. It seems all too clear that the mathematical idea of extrapolation can only be functionally effective in a restricted space in which all information is known. Critics feel it is all too apparent that every economic model must depict a sub-model of the overall economy. This in turn means that any claim of total simulation—of identifying every relevant measure, context, and decision-making variable (as well as the decision-making subjects), and depicting and

7   See for example Pias 2005 on the *Cybersyn* project.
8   See for example *Brooking III*, a Brookings Institution model that depicts macro- and microeconomics in equation-based simulations. Beginning in 1961, Brookings, an American think tank, presented three US national economy simulation models in rapid succession. The third model consisted of four hundred equations that were divided into eight sectors with the objective of enabling a time dynamic evaluation of the US gross national product (see Adelmann 1972, 214–220).
9   Sources repeatedly point out that in the last years of the postwar boom, a number of large enterprises in the USA and Europe put a lot of work into developing simulation models for short, medium, and long-term overall enterprise planning and aids to management decision-making processes (for example Amstutz and Claycamp 1964). One of the earliest Bsims to come out of the Federal Republic of Germany, the *Bull/OMNILOG* game, used the promise of such a total simulation in its advertising (Bull 1960).

quantifying their respective interdependencies—is doomed to fail (for example Sieber 1963, 83–87)—much like Borges' mile-to-mile map.[10]

Simulation Euphoria and Limiting the Future

No matter how we conceptualize the specific manifestation of Bsims and management simulation games, in an epistemological sense, they appear to be closely connected to limiting uncertainties. Regardless of whether we consider decision-making assistance systems, training simulations in the field of development, or the fantasy of total enterprise simulation—all these examples seem to focus on controlling the future (or rather on making contingency controllable). All these different methods (also) always aim to limit the contingency of this future. Above all, the various practices are characterized (and held together) by a specific type of rationality that, in the broadest sense, could be gathered under the umbrella term of "predictability." This rationality is supported considerably by the ideal computer constellation, which, during this period of time, is considered a promise of objective feasibility due to its computing calculations.[11] All in all, over the relatively short period of twenty to thirty years, a "decisively heterogeneous collection of the most

10 This (paradoxical) map that depicts the territory at a scale of 1:1, or, in other words, without any kind of reduction, is found throughout literary history, from Lewis Carroll to Umberto Eco. The most well-known version is possibly that of Jorge Luis Borges (1975): "Of Exactitude in Science" (In: *Universal History of Infamy*, Penguin Books, London).

11 If we look at early computing projects and approaches in the period following the end of World War II, one metaphor stands out: namely that of the computer as an electronic brain. In the following years, this metaphor shaped the debate on computers—it significantly represents the techno-euphoric exaggerations attributed to computers (at least in the common sense) (for example Schwarte-Amedick 2005, 68; see Nohr 2019, Chapter 7 in more detail).

varied knowledge systems"[12] culminated in a specific and more superordinate knowledge constellation, represented by management simulations. Not least, this constellation opened up a sphere of action that was to minimize contingency and establish the ability to control the future—on a purely operational level.

In this context, one does not need to refer exclusively to the fantasy of total enterprise simulation but can go through the Bsims training instruments (a much more pragmatic approach) to see how, in a paradigmatic, epistemological operation, the process of modeling and simulation has reshaped "historic facts" and "the present situation" into something that depicts "the now" while at the same time promising to hold the extension of said now within itself, namely "the future." At the same time, the construction of this "now" was encouraged to enable players to limit the plurality of the future by selecting the right decision, in turn allowing them to reduce the multitude of possible futures to a collection of manageable future scenarios by means of a method of rational reduction. Such thinking understands the current condition of an economic system as the result of a former condition and the cause of the condition to follow—a logic that quickly tempts us to jump to "false naturalistic conclusions" by concluding what should be based on what is. This would not only summarize early simulation euphoria in a few handy bulletpoints, it would also paraphrase Pierre-Simon Laplace, who, in his 1814 *Essai philosophique sur les probabilités,* speculated whether the course of the world is founded on a system that, if known, would enable a mathematically gifted demon to unambiguously calculate his future based on the current state of the universe. In mathematics, all it takes are the "insults" of the three-body problem, the theory of relativity, or the quantum theory[13] to put Laplace's demon out of work and return the world to its

12   To be read in this context as a paraphrase of the renowned dispositive definition according to Foucault.

13   In other disciplines, this role was assumed by the theory of evolution, the theory of autopoietic systems, and psychoanalysis, to name a few.

potentially contingent state. Economics, on the other hand, requires the *Limits to Growth* calculation.

The climax (or hubris) of simulation euphoria was the 1972 report *The Limits to Growth* issued by the Club of Rome,[14] which received a mixed assessment from the public and experts. In one interpretation, the model seemed to be the logical consequence and ultimate implementation of the concept of the ability to model the future and derive decisions on operative actions for the present.[15] Interpreting as a prognostic model in such a way quickly leads to discussions on the accuracy of the algorithm, the data, and the model construction with the corresponding functionalization of the respective arguments. On the other hand, however, the model was considered and interpreted as a sensitivity model: an exploration of spheres of possibilities, a simple what-if question. When flipped thusly, the *Limits to Growth* approach marks the end of the (extremely naive and unabashedly euphoric) idea of the potentially endless ability to simulate every possible future.

14   The Club of Rome was founded by Italian industrialist Aurelio Peccei and others in 1968. Peccei aimed to set up an informal association that was to become a rather diffusely defined circle "… to advance three core ideas … a global and a long-term perspective, and the concept of *'problematique,'* a cluster of intertwined global problems." Club of Rome. 2019. "About us." Accessed September 13, 2019. https://www.clubofrome.org/about-us.

15   The *Limits to Growth* report (1972), which was compiled on behalf of the Club of Rome and financed by the Volkswagen Foundation, was primarily authored by Donella and Dennis Meadows and their employee, Jay Forrester. Forrester's system dynamics approach provided the fundamental, methodological tools. The report, which aimed to extrapolate the future of the global economy, used a system dynamics approach in its system analysis and subsequent (computer) simulation. The simulation examined the development of five tendencies that had been defined as central under various starting conditions and using a varying range of more economic data and key indicators. These five tendencies were: population growth, capital investments, raw material resources, agricultural investments, and pollution (Forrester 1972, 38).

 While today, *The Limits to Growth* is considered more objectively as the starting point for a criticism of the growth concept,

> "back then, many conservative critics considered it scientific quackery, which ... only found as many readers as it did thanks to the respective publisher's good—and, as it were, disastrous—marketing and now threatened to accelerate the already too pronounced, performance-reducing trend towards more "quality of life" as well as the general decline in values among youths...." (Bossmann 1995, 34–35)

However, the critical debate around the report is not merely a political debate but also a criticism of the method of simulatability and calculability, or in other words, an argument in favor of their reformulation (for example Nelson 1974, 68–69). The discourse on the functionality of prognostic methods somewhat lacks examples that could prove that (computer-based) simulation and modeling methods can predict the future with a high rate of accuracy and quantitative numbers. The Shell oil crisis report's much-cited accuracy entered folklore precisely because it is one of the few available positive examples of the evident effectiveness of scenario techniques.[16]

The Club of Rome report therefore launched two things. First, a critical discussion of the idea of the predictability of the future. The report did more than just prove to the Western world that growth is not limitless. Second, however, it also initiated a change

---

16   In the 1960s, Royal Dutch Shell AG established a scenario department headed by Pierre Wack. In one of the first scenarios presented to management, the department predicted a global oil (price) crisis. Based on that narrative, management initially discussed fictional operative countermeasures. When the Yom Kippur war erupted in October 1973, resulting in the Arab states consciously throttling oil drilling, which in turn led to an exponential increase in oil prices, the company was able to fall back on this scenario. Decision-makers within Shell were able to react swiftly and systematically to the situation (Wack 1985). The experience legitimized the scenario department at Shell—and this prime example has in turn legitimized the scenario technique to this day.

in the ability to operationalize prognostic methods that were supported by the "rationality of predictability" mentioned at the beginning. The report represented both the peak and the tipping point of the ability to operationalize methods that aim to make the future controllable in the present—in abstract and less prognostic terms.

The range of historical examples this text touches upon shows how the knowledge of operational prognostics is geared towards producing the future. The resulting ways of acting and thinking are largely abstract and future-orientated—or to be more precise, tailored to the creation of a specific future (or at least a manageable number of futures). Actions within model spheres, in simulation games, in practice simulations and scenario funnels always strive to defuse (threatening) contingencies of the future. Planners always want to be teleologists. Whether teleology is capable of taming contingencies remains to be seen. However, there are grounds to suspect that contingencies are more than an open sphere of the future that can be tamed by the exact and full assessment of the possible. Or to put it more bluntly: the (uncertain) future imploded into a kind of "feedback-effected present" in which tendencies are intensified or subdued. The future was hedged and immobilized.

The real and far stronger consequence of the first phase of simulations that led to the modeling euphoria between the 1950s and 1970s is perhaps the establishment of abstract measures—including the new "planning concept," the concept of "strategic controllability" or the concept of the "configurative." These rather abstract concepts could serve as much clearer markers of how the specific rationality revealed itself in the context of mathematical game theory, computer-based calculations and modeling processes. This movement, which steers away from concrete predictions of the future and turns towards the concept of limiting the future via a collection of forms of knowledge and actions to an extent that at least results in manageability, is— metaphorically speaking—the same as transitioning from using a crystal ball to tell the future (which tells us exactly what will happen tomorrow) to using an oracle (that requires us to provide our own interpretation of the action directives of tomorrow). And this mid-1970s shift in "contingency-minimizing techniques" has continued up to today.

Translated by Emma Jane Stone

Refereneces

Adelman, Irma. 1972. "Economic System Simulation in Business System Simulations." In *Simulation in Social and Administrative science. Overviews and case-examples*, edited by Harold Guetzkow, Philip Kotler, and Randall L. Schultz, 210–25. Englewood Cliffs, NJ: Prentice-Hal.

Amstutz, Arnold E., and Henry J. Claycamp. 1964. "The Total Market Environment Simulation—An Approach to Management Education." *Industrial Management Review* (5) 2: 47–60.

Andlinger, Gerhard R. 1958. "Business Games – Play One". *Harvard Business Review* 36 (2): 115–25.

Assa, Isak. 1982. "Management Simulation Games for Education and Research: A Comparative Study of Gaming in the Socialist Countries." *Simulation & Gaming* (13) 4: 379–412.

Bossmann, Jürgen. 1995. "Arrested Development: Obsessionen im Wachstumsdenken." In *Obsessionen: Beherrschende Gedanken im wissenschaftlichen Zeitalter*, edited by Michael Jeissmann, 26–78. Frankfurt am Main: Suhrkamp.

Brainard, William C., and Herbert E. Scarf. 2000. *How to Compute Equilibrium Prices in 1891*. Cowles Foundation Discussion Papers No. 1272.

Bröckling, Ulrich. 2007. *Das unternehmerische Selbst: Soziologie einer Subjektivierungsform*. Frankfurt am Main: Suhrkamp.

Bull. 1960. *Das BULL-Unternehmensspiel*. Köln: Exacta-Continental Büromaschinenwerk.

Burstein, Frada, and Clyde Holsapple. 2008. *Handbook on Decision Support Systems 1. Basic Themes*. Berlin: Springer.

Busse von Colbe, Walther, and Manfred Perlitz. 1978. "Zehn Jahre General Management-Fortbildung am Universitätsseminar der Wirtschaft." In *Lebenslanges Lernen,* edited by Horst Albach, Walther Busse von Colbe, and Hermann Sabel. 143–63. Wiesbaden: Gabler.

Cohen, Kalman J., and Eric Rhenman. 1961. "The Role of Management Games in Education and Research." *Management Science* (7) 2: 131–66.

Engelbart, Douglas C. 1962. *Augmenting Human Intellect: A Conceptual Framework*. SRI Project No. 3578. Summary Report. Stanford Research Institute, Menlo Park.

Engelbart, Douglas C., and William K. English. 1968. "A Research Center for Augmenting Human Intellect." In *AFIPS Conference Proceedings of the 1968 Fall Joint Computer Conference,* Vol. 33, 395–410: San Francisco, CA. https://doi.org/10.1145/1476589.1476645.

Fessler, Max E., Charles B. Saunders, and Jack D. Steele. 1959. *National Symposium on Management Games: Proceedings of the National Symposium on Management Games.* Edited by the Center for Research in Business. Lawrence: University of Kansas.

Forrester, Jay Wright. 1971. *World Dynamics.* Cambridge, MA: Wright-Allen.

Forrester, Jay Wright. 1972. *Der teuflische Regelkreis. Das Globalmodell der Menschheitskrise.* Stuttgart: DtV.

Giesen, Günter. 1967. „Digitale Simulation und Stochastische Entscheidungsprozesse." PhD diss., University of Cologne.

Grüne-Yanoff, Till, and Paul Weirich 2010. "The Philosophy and Epistemology of Simulation: A Review." *Simulation & Gaming* (41) 3: 20–50.

Kahn, Hermann. 1960. *On Thermonuclear War.* Princeton: Princeton University Press.

Koller, Horst. (1966) 1975. "Simulation als Methode in der Betriebswirtschaft." In Grundlagen der Wirtschafts- und Sozialkybernetik: Betriebswirtschaftliche Kontrolltheorie, edited by Jörg Baetge, 165–78. Wiesbaden: VS Verlag für Sozialwissenschaften.

Luhmann, Niklas. 2018. *Organization and Decision,* edited by Dirk Baecker and Rhodes Barrett, Cambridge, MA: Cambridge University Press.

Nelson, Theodor H. 1974. *Computer Lib: You Can and Must Understand Computers Now / Dream Machines: New Freedoms Through Computer Screens— A Minority Report.* Self published.

Neumann, John von, and Oskar Morgenstern. 1944. *Theory of Games and Economic Behavior.* Princeton: Princeton University Press.

Newell, William T., and Robert C. Meier. 1972. "Business System Simulations." In *Simulation in Social and Administrative Science: Overviews and Case-Examples,* edited by Harold Guetzkow, Philip Kotler, and Randall L. Schultz, 415–58. Englewood Cliffs, NJ: Prentice-Hall.

Nohr, Rolf F. 2019. *Unternehmensplanspiele 1955–1975: Die Herstellung unternehmerischer Rationalität im Spiel.* In collaboration with Tobias Conradi, Tim Glaser, Kerstin Hoffmann, and Theo Röhle. Münster: LiT.

Pias, Claus. 2005. "Der Auftrag. Kybernetik und Revolution in Chile." In *Politiken der Medien,* edited by Daniel Gethmann, 131–53. Zürich: Diaphanes.

Ricciardi, Franc M., Clifford J. Craft, Donald G. Malcolm, Richard Bellman, Charles Clark, Joel M. Kibbee, and Richard Rawdon. 1957. *Top Management Simulation: The AMA Approach.* New York: American Management Association.

Rühl, Günther. 1961. "Die Rolle der unternehmerischen Planspiele in Ausbildung und Forschung: Nach K.J. Cohen und E. Rhenman, berichtet von Günther Rühl" *Fortschrittliche Betriebsführung* (11) 2: 33–39.

Sauermann, Heinz, and Reinhard Selten. 1959. "Ein Oligopolexperiment." *Zeitschrift für die gesamte Staatswissenschaft* (115) 3: 427–64.

Schmidt, Ernst. 1963. "Univac-Unternehmensspiele." *Die Lochkarte* (27) 9: 25–35.

98   Schwarte-Amedick, Margret. 2005. "Von papierlosen Büros und menschenleeren Fabriken." In *Zukünfte des Computers*, edited by Claus Pias, 67–86. Zürich: Diaphanes.

Shubik, Martin. 1975. *Games for Society, Business and War: Towards a Theory of Gaming*. New York: Elsevier.

Sieber, Eugen H. 1963. "Das Planspiel unternehmerischer Entscheidungen." In *Betriebsführung und Operations Research*, edited by Adolf Angermann, 80–123. Frankfurt am Main: Novak.

Stachowiak, Herbert. 1973. *Allgemeine Modelltheorie*. Wien: Springer.

Wack, Pierre. 1985. "Scenarios: Shooting the Rapids." *Harvard Business Review*. November–December: 139–50.

Witte, Thomas. 1973. *Simulationstheorie und ihre Anwendung auf betriebliche Systeme*. Wiesbaden: Gabler.

ANTHROPOCENE

NEGOTIATION ZONES

SPACES OF THOUGHT

AISTHESIS

PRACTICES

4

Opening Futures

Irina Kaldrack

The purpose of this paper is to shed light on the ways contemporary humanities and media theorists open up negotiation zones for desirable futures. A desirable future in terms of transformation design is understood as one that secures biodiversity and human survival and improves global justice. The issue is the facilitation of sustainable futures and how such futures might be conceptualizable and negotiable. The discursive background of the Anthropocene is used to explore and examine the way media studies discourses and theory development could inform and support transformational design practice and research.

102 In the conceptualization and negotiation of desirable futures in terms of transformation design, the relationship between theory and practice is particularly relevant to understanding and dealing with nature. A critical core element of the political concept of sustainability (regardless of which specific formulation) is the question of who has which power of disposal over which life-forms and resources. The concept of sustainability was given a political formulation for the first time in the UN's World Commission on Environment and Development (WCED) 1987 Brundtland Report: "Sustainable development is development that meets the needs of the present without compromising the ability of future generations to meet their own needs" (WCED 1987, 54). A three-pillar model of sustainable development in which ecological, social, and economic dimensions are intertwined was gradually recognized as a realizable political model in the 1990s. The same concept is reflected in the 17 sustainable development goals adopted by the United Nations in 2016.

In such formulations and formalizations, sustainability is, firstly, an anthropocentric concept. It is about the needs of people. The central focus is, however, secondly, justice between people—it is primarily about the needs of disadvantaged people and societies, i.e., equal opportunity and participation as well as economic and environmental justice. Thirdly, the goal of limiting demand is resource conservation and environmental protection, and fourthly, inherent in the concept of sustainability is a reference to the future. Sustainability is revealed to be a future-oriented concept that is, at its core, normative and positions humans in relation to nature. To negotiate desirable futures, it is then necessary to clarify the following questions. How are standard needs defined? Whose needs are they? Which needs are they? And what sort of relationship is consequently contoured between humans, nature, and culture?

There are many intersections between the concepts and realities of sustainability and digital cultures in the past and present. I will outline their entanglement in terms of epistemologies,

economies, and knowledge cultures as a basis to discuss the
question of negotiation zones for desirable futures.

Firstly, sustainability discourses and digital culture discourses
have overlapping origins and are intertwined in many ways. The
connections are particularly evident in concepts such as dynamic
systems, complexity, and emergence. Gaia is a particularly
impressive example. It is based on (bio)cybernetic concepts,
which are relevant to environmental systems science and connect
to more recent discourse in the humanities and media studies
centered on the Anthropocene[1] and political economies.[2] Central to this discursive intersection is that both the relationship
between humans and their "natural" environment and humans
and their technological environments are thought of as embeddedness and interaction. Following on from that, the spheres of
sustainability and digital cultures share certain problems and
raise similar questions. The conditions of interconnectedness and
distributedness, in particular, give rise to urgent questions about
the status of decisions, actions, and responsibility. Questions
of historiography also arise in the debate about and shaping of
sustainability. Questions about how the climate and biodiversity crises have come about, global injustices, and exploitative
relationships between people, between societies, and between
societies and the biosphere simultaneously nominate points of
action.

1   The concept of the Anthropocene concept is that we are currently living in an
     age in which humans are having a decisive (if unintentional) influence on the
     shape of the Earth's surface and on processes of the biosphere, lithosphere,
     hydrosphere, and atmosphere. Popularized in 2000 by Paul Crutzen and
     Eugene Stoermer, the concept is intensely debated in the geosciences and
     the humanities, particularly the fact that it is anthropocentric, i.e., human
     centered. See, for example, the new *Future Ecologies* series from meson
     press, edited by Petra Löffler, Claudia Mareis and Florian Sprenger (2021).
2   On the reception of Gaia, with its multiple overlaps between bio-cybernetic,
     esoteric, and evolutionary metaphors and discourses, see Friedrich (2018).
     For Stenger's use of the Gaia concept, see below.

104 *Secondly*, it can then be stated that digital technologies and the cultures that accompany them are a problem in many areas when it comes to sustainable futures. Resources for the production and operation of digital technologies—including rare earth metals—are neither ecologically nor socially sustainable. As plundered natural resources, they are the basis of exploitative relationships globally and locally. Large amounts of electricity are required for operation; large amounts of CO_2 and other byproducts are produced. Digital economies—from high-frequency stock trading to so-called platform capitalism and click-work—reinforce existing dynamics in terms of oligopolization on a global level (and within specific continents and regions of the world), social inequality and income distribution on a national and global level. Furthermore, digital cultures reinforce power relationships and cultural hegemonies even when marginalized people and groups can, conversely, network and make their discourse public and heard by large numbers of people. It is striking that infrastructures and digital methods (of computing, as well as the accumulation and evaluation of such data) tend to be used universalistically, while diversity and particularity are more often reflected at content level.[3] *Thirdly* the reverse is also true: sustainability would be difficult to achieve without digital cultures. Partly because it is very unlikely that digital technologies and their networking capabilities will ever disappear or stop being used. And partly because everything we know about the biosphere, the climate, and the myriad meta-crises is based on specific digital cultures—infrastructures, practices of computation, calculations with models and simulations, representation forms of results in climate images, scientific networks, and struggles for interpretive sovereignty are all central to climate knowledge in particular.[4] Negotiation zones for desirable futures shift against

3   Distelmeyer provides an overview of the current mélange of technical logics, myth, and infrastructural materialities, and the temporalities and dynamics of "digitality" in the first chapter of his book *Critique of Digitality* (2022).

4   See Edwards (2010), Gramelsberger (2010), Gabrys (2016).

this background of entangled epistemologies of sustainability,
digital cultures, and contemporary socio-technological politics
and economies. In that context, analyses of current crises and
dynamics, especially ecological crises, are crucial in reference
to the future. Any understanding about how these crises will
develop in the future is heavily influenced by simulations—that
is, by data and its conversion into models. Similarly, the concepts
of complexity and dynamic systems raise questions about the
unplanned effects of decisions and actions in socio-technological-
material frameworks. One of the greatest challenges is that
climate change is, on the one hand, a global event and knowledge
object that needs to be dealt with globally, and from that perspective, a universal rationality is imperative. On the other hand,
our global knowledge of "climate," as well as all our actions and
decisions, are based on data that is anchored locally (Gabrys
2016). The slogan "think globally, act locally" emphasizes *one*
dimension of this entanglement, making it readable as a subject-
technology of a specific climate regime that calls for action as
subjectively eco-socially correct behavior. "Think globally" refers
to the universal rationality that ideally guides the subjective
action; "act locally" incorporates that universal rationality and
actualizes it on a locally situated, embodied level. In this universalistic approach, a second dimension of entanglement is lost,
namely that both (implicit) climate knowledge and climate change
consequences are locally situated and that this situatedness
and entanglement with local behaviors and actions are hardly
ever included in the data collection, models, and simulations, if
at all.[5] In the following discussion, I will talk about three writers
who problematize different aspects and dimensions of current
regimes of thought and action in the context of ecological crises,
social injustice (on a global scale), and their embeddedness in
global economies. Isabelle Stengers (2015), Amitav Ghosh (2016),
and Donna Haraway (2016) call for new narratives, epistemes, and
practices on the basis of their findings. They strongly suggest that

5   See Schneider and Walsh (2019), Löffler et al. (2020).

 "business-as-usual" is no longer possible in the face of the threat of world problems/the climate crisis. Something has to change.

Each of the three writers characterize the prevailing "human–world" reference as problematic and call for new forms of reference between human and world that must go hand-in-hand with new forms of perception and corresponding practices. They each take somewhat different approaches, which I will briefly outline. Finally, I will examine how these considerations can and should become fruitful for the zones of negotiation in focus here.

Isabelle Stengers: In Catastrophic Times

Isabelle Stengers' book looks at ways to resist a coming barbarism. It is about the foreseeable, catastrophic consequences of climate change and its impact on human society, including the possible extinction of humans. Though the situation worsened in the years between the publication of the French original in 2009 and the release of an English translation in 2015, government technologies, according to Stengers, did not change in spite of the impending climate catastrophe. Her analysis is an explanation of the issue and potential tactics of resistance.

Stengers uses the metaphor and concept of Gaia. She describes the current situation of increasingly extreme weather such as storms, floods, droughts and the resulting forest fires as the "Intrusion of Gaia" an invasion or incursion of Gaia into the reality of human societies. Stengers consciously places her work in the tradition of James Lovelock and Lynn Margulis, and conceptualizes Gaia *as if* it were an organism, an organism whose self-organization, however, is to be thought of non-teleologically.[6] According to Stengers, this conceptualization calls for a new way of thinking about the relationship between humans and the biosphere. The biosphere is "a ticklish assemblage of forces that are

6   See Stengers (2015, 43–50). On the status of as if or As-if see Friedrich (2018, 49–59, particularly the section on Gaia's networks).

indifferent to our reasons and our projects" (Stengers 2015, 47).
Her analysis starts with the observation that the intrusion of Gaia
has not altered the premise of capitalist growth, even though in
2015—and even more so in 2021—there is widespread consensus
that the models of production of global capitalism, as well as
the ways of life in the Global North, are fueling climate change.
Stengers attributes the cause to what she calls the capitalist
machine. "Capitalism must be understood instead as a mode of
functioning, a machine, which fabricates its own necessity, its
own actors, in every conjuncture, and destroys those who haven't
been able to saddle up for the new opportunities" (52).

The functioning of capitalism-as-machine is characterized by the
fact that the value of everything is determined by money and is
potentially seen as a source of profit. Progress is the value, tran-
scendence, and even drive that keeps the machine running. More
specifically, an ideology of expansion that relies on innovation
and productivity growth. There are three corresponding positions
with specific modes of action: the State, the Entrepreneur and
Science.

The state as an institutionalized form of rule is responsible for
protecting and caring for the population, which is achieved
through the legal and institutional regulation of human relations,
the concrete forms of which are negotiated politically. However,
the State increasingly dominates the population through technocratic management justified by the need for progress and its
TINA—"there is no alternative"—logic. The Entrepreneur in turn
is "he for whom everything is an opportunity, or rather, he who
demands the freedom to be able to transform everything into
an opportunity for new profits, including what calls the common
future into question" (Stengers 2015, 65).

The Entrepreneur develops and sells goods and services. The
actor-position is characterized by seeing everything as an opportunity (for profit), externalizing disadvantages, and demanding
(from the state and society) the right to non-responsibility.

 Science mediates between the state's concern for the community and non-responsibility by carrying out risk assessments for new technological processes. Moreover, Science develops new knowledge and new processes—financed by the state—which are then turned into profit by the Entrepreneurs.

In capitalism-as-machine, these three actor entities interact in such a way that market dynamics, at the core of which is progress, are not disturbed. The right of non-responsibility ensures that the disadvantages and (ecological) costs are externalized and disappear from public consciousness.

The task now, according to Stengers, is to throw sand in the gears of capitalism-as-machine. It needs to be infiltrated and opposed with alternative function logic. We have to disrupt the naturalized connection between progress and profit and develop forms of resistance against it. For Stengers, "the political" as a question of collective decision-making modes and confrontational negotiation of interests is central.

The concept of Gaia is fundamental to Stengers' strategy. Gaia should be thought of as a collection of non-human forces, completely uninfluenced by human motivations and actions; humans cannot communicate with Gaia, cannot address her as an authority or entity. Stengers outlines what *Faire-Attention*, the art of paying-attention, might be like—something that prioritizes the common good, questions the logic of technocratic management, and draws attention to (calls out) stupidity.

It is a matter of first disrupting the logic of argumentation and power regimes by raising enough opposition to the introduction of "innovations" such as genetically modified organisms. Asking the right questions to expose actor's lines of argumentation and countering with alternatives is essential. Some examples could be questions like: Who profits? What are the consequences? Who pays for the damage? (Stengers 2015, 40). And the whole process needs to happen in such a way that political collectives form around each problem. It is imperative that more and different

knowledge is produced as an alternative to the knowledge
belonging to the association of Entrepreneur, State and Science.
The extent that "scientific" knowledge follows interests—for
example when studies by industry players are made or commis-
sioned—must be exposed. It needs activism and, in this case, an
intervention, a decontamination. Partly to prevent contamination
of other organisms in the short term, and partly to generate
attention. And finally, political momentum is required to build
the majorities required for decision making. Stengers' attention is
directed specifically toward Science, which she sees as having an
obligation to fit research and development into a socio-ecological
context and formulate questions that are less oriented toward
technological solutions.

With reference to Stengers, negotiation zones should be spaces
or zones that are, in a sense, wrested from the regime of capitalism-as-machine. They should follow a different internal logic
than that of the machine and its actors regarding the *problem*
being dealt with. The first task is developing questions that
adequately address the issue, making the existing logic visible
and problematizing it. It is necessary to develop a practice of
faire attention; in other words, it is important to develop social
attention and mindfulness of the problem in connection with the
questions. On that basis, practices or tactics should be found
that (can), firstly, disrupt dealings with capitalism-as-machine,
and secondly, those that can answer the problem in question
with Gaia. However, according to writer Amitav Ghosh, that would
require other forms of imaginary and narration.

Ghosh: The Great Derangement

In his essay "The Great Derangement. Climate Change and the
Unthinkable," Amitav Ghosh questions the relationship between
climate change and narrative. He explains how the interlocking
of narrative and thought patterns is situated in the context of a
specific world model and understanding of nature. The result is

 clarification of the way that world model is based on imperialism as a global form of power and is secured by (the victor's) historical narrative.

Ghosh's starting point is his observation that "climate change" is a topic that literary fiction rarely engages with. Referring to literary journals such as *London Review of Books*, *The New York Review of Books*, and *Los Angeles Review of Books*, he points out that in regard to the canon of "serious literature journals," (from the mid-2010s): "the mere mention of the subject is often enough to relegate a novel or a short story to the genre of science fiction. It is as though in the literary imagination climate change were somehow akin to extraterrestrials or interplanetary travel" (Ghosh 2016, 7). Ghosh argues that the emergence of the "realistic novel" in the first half of the nineteenth century follows a regime of continuity of plausibility, even probability. While there are surprises, adventures, and disruptive events, the foil of the event is a fundamental orderliness in which improbability is on the extreme end of the spectrum of probability. That attitude, in turn, corresponds with the emerging "range of governmental practices that were informed by statistics and probability" (25).

Ghosh develops his characterization of the subject form in realistic novels based on a review by John Updike, according to which "that sense of individual moral adventure—of the evolving individual in varied and roughly equal battle with a world of circumstance—which since 'Don Quixote' and 'Robinson Crusoe,' has distinguished the novel from the fable and the chronicle" (77).

Accordingly, a realistic novel establishes a subject that acts or tries to act in an effective way in relation to a natural world that is passive, and in doing so undergoes inner—which usually means psychological—development.

This shapes a mode of experience in fictional literature which in turn corresponds to a specific analytical and rational form of thinking. Such a form of thinking understands nature as something that doesn't make any big leaps, and also follows a

specific understanding of natural history that was fiercely fought
over at the beginning of the nineteenth century.

There were two opposing schools of thought in the emerging disciplines of paleontology and geology of the time, catastrophism, and gradualism or actualism. In catastrophism, the assumption is that the earth's development and evolution are decisively shaped by catastrophic events and thus emphasize the improbable and extraordinary "behavior" of nature. In contrast the basic assumption in actualism is that geological processes progress uniformly. The processes are subject to laws that are thought to be continuous. In paleontological practice, this basic assumption allows us to make inferences about the history of the earth and past life forms from geological formations and fossils.

With regard to the social situation, the nineteenth century industrial revolution, the formation of a specific capitalism, and—critically for Ghosh—imperialism and a specific form of globalization are decisive. These developments were formative for the current climate crisis. In relation to Ghosh's question about the interlocking of narration and thought patterns, this perspective reveals the way written history is a very specific historiography of victors.

The history of progress is frequently constructed by written history—especially the state historiography that was common in the nineteenth century, but also technological history—the messy narrative is made clean. Ghosh illustrates this with selected historical spotlights on petroleum uses and economies in South and Southeast Asia. Such lines of industrial history, Ghosh argues, fall outside the purifying historiography that narrates the modern Western development myth. In the process, imperialist forms of power and domination that subjugate regions, nations, and people to technological-economic development are destabilized.

Aisthesis—in the sense of perception, representation, ways of thinking, and specific forms of governance—participate in and fuel a regime in which specific conceptions of subject, nature, and historiographies are formed, and that are still influential today. It is particularly evident in politics, which, according to Ghosh, has in recent years centered on the moral individual. Politics is—from the perspective of 2016—an "'individual moral adventure' in the sense of being an interior journey guided by the conscience" (Ghosh 2016, 127). Accordingly, the focus is on individuals, their sincerity, and their authenticity. State power and political decisions are strongly influenced by the elite and institutions, while the public and public opinion—though they have become far more open, differentiated, and diverse—now have only a dwindling influence.

Building on this analysis, Ghosh calls for a new form of (literary) imaginary to provide experiences and narratives that could make new and climate-change appropriate possibilities for thought and action conceivable. This new or re-established imaginary fiction form needs to expand collective decision making and action, allow non-human agents and actors to (re)appear, and make other possible forms of existence imaginable. Only then are we able to see how and by whom collective political decisions are made and how global, distributive justice oriented toward the common good can be achieved.

In light of these arguments, negotiation zones in terms of transformation design should start with the analysis of hidden logics that are relevant to the problem being discussed. Ghosh points to the longue durée of such logics, which connect imperialism, historiography, and specific (rational) forms of thinking and subject forms. In order to open these up, it is necessary to develop imaginaries that make other forms of thinking possible. One form could be to follow destabilized histories and, building on them, question prevailing subject forms. Central to that, Ghosh indicates, is the development of narrative forms that make other subject positions and forms of action conceivable. In other words, negotiating other forms of thinking that enable different rationalities, imagine other forms-of-being and ideally situate them particularlistically instead of universalistically. In zones of negotiation, it is critical that forms of power and subjectivity of the longue durée be thematized, and that the trap of authenticity and morality be avoided.

Haraway: Staying with the Trouble

Donna Haraway also stresses that the prevailing world view is a failure. To meet the current challenges in the face of global injustice, species extinction, and climate change, it is simply no longer appropriate to believe that "humans" occupy the "pre-eminent position" in this world. Common concepts such as "individuality" and "self" are no help either, because they are contaminated with a specifically human-centered rationality and power. Abstract thinking that negates entanglement with the material-political world legitimizes and reinforces everyday thoughtlessness in action. So, it is necessary to examine,

> What happens when human exceptionalism and bounded individualism, those old saws of Western philosophy and political economics, become unthinkable in the best science, whether natural or social? Seriously unthinkable: not available to think with. (Haraway 2016, 57)

Haraway's explanations focus on epistemes, metaphors, and practices (primarily artistic) to configure our relation to the world anew. *Staying with the Trouble* outlines approaches to thinking and acting that enable alternative ways of relating to the world and to each other, which should be fundamentally characterized by responsibility and care for and about the world. Haraway's proposal—and book subtitle—is *Making Kin in the Chthulucene*. It is necessary to develop a thinking space that creates binding, interspecies communities and so promotes becoming responsible as much as becoming able to respond.

For questions about the contouring of zones of negotiation, spaces of thought and practices that I am interested in, some of the strategies Haraway employs to unravel material-semiotic knots, take up the threads, and weave them seem particularly relevant. For example, she is concerned with which stories tell history(s). Metaphors such as Humus not Humanism interrogate powerful traditions of thought and call for new practices of thinking. "Human as humus has potential, if we could chop and shred human as Homo, the detumescing project of a self-making and planet-destroying CEO" (Haraway 2016, 32).

With conceptual creations like critter, tentacular, the Earth-bound, and the Chthulucene, Haraway links biological bodies of knowledge with myths and metaphorical bodies of knowledge. She begins with the spider *Pimoa cthulhu*, whose name is a reference to the Cthulhu Mythos invented by H.P. Lovecraft. Haraway doesn't, however, explicitly refer to the Lovecraft world, and shifts an "h" to the beginning of the spider's name. In her interpretation, chthulu is connected to the Greek Chthonioi—the gods of the underworld and the Titans. The superimposition of the spider, the tentacular, and deities on the chthonic figure of Medusa enables Haraway to recontextualize forms of knowledge and power shaped by myths by reconstructing the pre-Greek (Minoan) genealogies of those myths (in this case the Minoan goddess Potnia Theron).[7] Furthermore, Haraway refers to hidden histories that are dealt with in feminist speculative fiction.[8] Similarly, she invokes the scientific concept of sympoiesis.[9] The key feature of the theory is that evolutionary development can result from a union of "mutually alien" organisms, and perhaps this happens even quite frequently. This means "becoming-with" must be considered in ecosystems, and sympoiesis is a concept to think the ways that "becoming-with" can and should happen.

7   See "Chthulucene" (Haraway 2016, 51–57).

8   On feminist speculation, see Angerer and Gramlich (2020).

9   Sympoiesis—developed by the evolutionary biologist Lynn Margulis, who developed the Gaia hypothesis with James Lovelock—is a concept that ties in with what is known as endosymbiont theory or symbiogenesis. According to endosymbiont theory, in the process of evolution certain unicellular organisms entered into symbiotic communities, which led to new organisms.

Such thought and concept work are situated precisely within a 115
certain epistemic space. In that space, it undergoes shifts and inversions that open up new traditions and genealogies in equal measure, as well as carrying the classical lines along in some way. The point is to show possibilities of thinking, to bring concepts and terms into the world for a specific scope of application.

These thought spaces and claims to validity are related to practices of response-ability,[10] caring for and about kin, and kin-making. It is important to establish carefully claims of validity and test actions as response-able actions that are always simultaneously active *and* passive, or at least alternately active and passive.

Haraway highlights art practice as an example of a practice that creates relationships and establishes intimacy without proximity. Key practices are those that are collective, create connection, establish references between strangers narratively, are capable of representing interests and agency of other species. Such practices need to be situated but also very reflexive with regard to the context, relationships, and power structures in which they are embedded. Ideally, they then enable the construction of niches in which people and other living beings can live worth- while, connected lives.

Haraway's analysis shows—in a similar way to Ghosh's—that human beings as a species, the concept of the autonomous, rational subject, and the forms of abstract, thus unifying, thinking with claims to universal validity are part of the problem, not the solution. Her approach is to no longer conceptualize species and the subject/individual as a unity, sealed off from others, but to show ways to build relationships with others (and thus be involved and responsible for them). The practices and strategies arising from her approach are linked to power and

10   With the shift from responsibility to response-ability, Haraway connects accountability with a capacity to respond. See also Saskia Hebert's contribution in this volume.

 claims to validity. They should never be universalistic but always contextualized.

In light of Haraway's analysis, it can be concluded that transformation design negotiation zones must firstly be very clearly contoured. Like Stengers, Haraway makes the assumption that collectives form around problems. First, it is necessary to ask which actors, human and non-human, should be brought into the more-than-human fold, and who attends which concerns. It is necessary to sound out which concept(s) and metaphors can be used for speaking and thinking in order to respond to the problem and to answer with the relevant kin. And it is important to reconstruct and tell shared histories. Practices of observation, analysis, representation, and construction should be responseable, capable of responding to problems and those who are being-with. The form of action ideally emerges in togetherness and does justice to the materialities and respective contexts.

Conclusions, Connections, and Outlooks

Each of the writers presented reaches similar conclusions based on their respective analysis. In this summary, it is important to highlight the similarities, and reveal the reference shared by them. The differences between them, in my view, lie in where they each place emphasis. The current situation and the associated problems compel all three writers to, *firstly*, conduct in-depth analyses. The analyses are intended to reveal forms of thinking, power, and subjectivity that contribute to the crises and problems under consideration. Depending on their respective focus, the writers undertake historical analyses of concepts such as the human being as a species, historically developed subject forms, understandings of nature and science, but also the re-construction of contemporary societies and economies with their injustices and blind spots. The writers ask which exclusions and hierarchizations current normalities are based on. *Secondly*, all three point out that new forms of aisthesis are necessary—other

ways of perceiving the world, which also means other ways of
representing, depicting, narrating, and experiencing the world.
As engaged and situated aisthesis, it should be based on concern and responsiveness, working with attention and enabling
relationship building and kin making. It needs to be particularly
clear here that these are forces and actor-instances that do
not engage in discourses but can break into reality. Interwoven
with all this is, *thirdly*, the necessity of opening up new spaces of
thought that make it possible to ask questions in the first place
to design other, more adequate and more desirable futures.
Fourthly, new practices are needed, practices of speculating,
creating, and negotiating. It is important, in turn, that forms
of dissent, conflict, divergence, and difference exist and are
negotiated. Otherwise hardly anything new can emerge or be
tested. Insofar as these four aspects or dimensions are closely
intertwined, it also becomes clear that aesthetics is always ethics
and the decisive questions are those of claims to validity and
negotiation.

Admittedly the theories developed here, although developed
from practices, are not easy to translate into practices that—like
transformation design—support forms of action to bring sustainable futures into the world and make them effectively even
more sustainable. There is a gap between subjectivizing forms
of kin-making and strategies that prevent or at least slow down
increasing rises in sea levels.

In my opinion, the basis for transformation design negotiation
zones is the analysis of problems and their contexts. The thinkers
discussed here identify which dimensions need to be considered and how such analyses can be guided by values and norms.
Building on that, negotiation zones should be designed to relate
to the contexts and power relationships analyzed precisely;
designs can enable spaces and conditions to be created for actors
to shape their practices and relationships in open processes
to simultaneously develop and test new logics of thought and
action. Ideally, the actors are clear about the claim to validity of

 the zones and processes they design and reflect on their ways of thinking and practices with regard to the inclusions, exclusions and blind spots that appear in them.

It seems to me crucial that the design of such negotiation zones centers on negotiation practices and aesthetic-designing practices that are in turn reflexively related to external contexts and internal power relations. It is (also) important to consider that creativity practices in design have long been part of the tech innovation toolbox. Design thinking, speculative design, scenario analysis, and similar practices, as well as forms of experimentation, modulation, and criticism, are always integrated into regimes of digital cultures that fuel less desirable futures. Furthermore, I ask myself whether and to what extent negotiation forms developed following the theories of these three writers would be imagined in terms of moderation and coaching. When Ghosh argues for a literary imaginary to be developed and Haraway weaves entanglements based on artistic projects into epistemically functional connections, they are aiming for imaginative spaces and ways of thinking about (individual) subjects. In so far as Stengers develops her theory based on political activists, her aim is to change public discussion; the practices she outlines establish mutually supportive alliances. I ask myself whether the discourses, forms of perception and practices of attention, care, alliances, and strengthening shouldn't be accompanied by those of confrontation and conflict. How can dissent in community and society be endured and potentially, in the form of solidarity in dissent, made productive?

Translated by Janet Leyton-Grant

References

Angerer, Marie-Luise, and Naomie Gramlich. 2020. *Feministisches Spekulieren: Genealogien, Narrationen, Zeitlichkeiten*. Berlin: Kulturverlag Kadmos Berlin.
Distelmeyer, Jan. 2022. *Critique of Digitality*. Wiesbaden: Palgrave Macmillan.

Edwards, Paul N. 2010. *A Vast Machine: Computer Models, Climate Data, and the Politics of Global Warming.* Cambridge, MA: MIT Press.

Friedrich, Alexander. 2018. "Gaias Netze: Zur Metaphorologie der planetarischen Selbstregulation des Lebens." In *Ökologien der Erde: Zur Wissensgeschichte und Aktualität der Gaia-Hypothese*, edited by Alexander Friedrich, Petra Löffler, Niklas Schrape, and Florian Sprenger, 21–61. Lüneburg: meson press.

Gabrys, Jennifer. 2016. *Program Earth: Environmental Sensing Technology and the Making of a Computational Planet.* Minneapolis: University of Minnesota Press.

Gál, Réka Patrícia, and Petra Löffler. 2021. *Earth and Beyond in Tumultuous Times: A Critical Atlas of the Anthropocene.* Lüneburg: meson press.

Ghosh, Amitav. 2016. *The Great Derangement: Climate Change and the Unthinkable.* Chicago: University of Chicago Press.

Gramelsberger, Gabriele. 2010. *Computerexperimente: Zum Wandel der Wissenschaft im Zeitalter des Computers.* Bielefeld: transcript.

Haraway, Donna J. 2016. *Staying with the Trouble: Making Kin in the Chthulucene.* Durham, NC: Duke University Press.

Horn, Eva. 2014. *Zukunft als Katastrophe.* Frankfurt am Main: S. Fischer Verlag.

Indigenous Action. 2019. "Rethinking the Apocalypse: An Indigenous Anti-Futurist Manifesto." Accessed May 28, 2021. http://www.indigenousaction.org/rethinking-the-apocalypse-an-indigenous-anti-futurist-manifesto/.

Löffler, Petra, Léa Perraudin, Birgit Schneider, Kathryn Yusoff, and Jennifer Gabrys. 2020. "Dinge anders machen: Ein Gespräch über feministische Anthropozän-Kritik, Dekolonisierung der Geologie und 'sensing' in Medien-Umwelten." *Zeitschrift für Medienwissenschaft.* Heft 23: Zirkulation (12) 2: 138–52.

Schneider, Birgit, and Lynda Walsh. 2019. "The Politics of Zoom: Problems with Downscaling Climate Visualizations." *Geography and Environment* (6) 1: 1–11. https://doi.org/10.1002/geo2.70

Stengers, Isabelle. 2015. In *Catastrophic Times: Resisting the Coming Barbarism.* Translated by Andrew Goffey. London: Open Humanities Press in collaboration with meson press. https://doi.org/10.14619/016.

World Commission on Environment and Development. 1987. *Our Common Future: Report of the World Commission on Environment and Development.* United Nations Document A/42/427 (English). Accessed June 13, 2021. http://www.un-documents.net/ocf-02.htm.

Authors

Saskia Hebert is an architect and urban researcher at subsolar* architektur & stadtforschung in Berlin. She taught transformation design at Braunschweig University of Art from 2015 to 2020.

Wolfgang Jonas is a professor emeritus of design studies at the Institute for Design Research, Braunschweig University of Art.

Irina Kaldrack is a lecturer for "Society and Digitalization" at Bauhaus University, Weimar. She was full professor at the Foreign Studies College of Hunan Normal University in Changsha, China (spring semester, 2022) and was visting professor for "Knowledge Cultures in the Digital Age" at Braunschweig University of Art (2015–2021).

Rolf F. Nohr is a professor of media aesthetics and media culture at Braunschweig University of Art and a University of Arizona external affiliate.